SPECIAL COMMEMORATIVE EDITION

THUNDERSTRUCK

THE OKLAHOMA CITY THUNDER'S HISTORIC RUN TO THE 2025 NBA CHAMPIONSHIP

CHRISTINE TANNOUS/INDYSTAR

THE OKLAHOMAN

Champions
20

NATHAN J. FISH/THE OKLAHOMAN

THE LINEUP

Sports editor
Jeff Patterson

Deputy sports editor
Jacob Unruh

Assistant sports editor
Darla Smith

Reporters
Joel Lorenzi
Joe Mussatto
Jenni Carlson
Justin Martinez

Photographers
Nathan J. Fish
Sarah Phipps
Bryan Terry
Doug Hoke

Executive editor
Ray Rivera

Fact-checker
Sherrill Amo

Project coordinator
Gene Myers

Special thanks
Chris Thomas
Noah Amstadter
Clarissa Young
Josh Williams
Vanessa Cotton

Content packaged by Mojo Media, Inc.
Joe Funk: Editor
Jason Hinman: Creative Director

BRYAN TERRY/THE OKLAHOMAN

ABOUT THE BOOK: ***THUNDERSTRUCK*** condenses a year's worth of the world's best coverage of the Oklahoma City Thunder from The Oklahoman. Follow the Thunder at oklahoman.com. Order a print subscription at 877-987-2737. This book includes coverage from the USA TODAY Network, which includes The Oklahoman.

THE OKLAHOMAN

Copyright © 2025 by The Oklahoman

No part of this publication may be reproduced, stored in a retrieval system or transmitted in any form by any means, electronic, mechanical, photocopying or otherwise, without prior written permission of the publisher, Triumph Books LLC, 814 North Franklin Street, Chicago, Illinois 60610.

PRINTED IN U.S.A.
ISBN: 978-1-63727-989-2

Front and back cover photos by NATHAN J. FISH/THE OKLAHOMAN

This is an unofficial publication. This book is in no way affiliated with, licensed by or endorsed by the National Basketball Association or the Oklahoma City Thunder.

814 North Franklin Street • Chicago, Illinois 60610 • Phone: (312) 337-0747
www.triumphbooks.com

THUNDERSTRUCK

BRYAN TERRY/THE OKLAHOMAN

8

THE CHAMPS

In Year 17, the Oklahoma City Thunder stormed to the franchise's first NBA championship behind the league's youngest roster and its loudest fans at Paycom Center.

16

THE SEASON

One for the ages: A franchise record for victories (68), the biggest point differential in NBA history (12.9 a game) and 50-point games by Shai Gilgeous-Alexander (4).

32

THE TEAM

From SGA's MVP award to Jalen Williams' star turn to Chet Holmgren's courageous return from a fractured pelvis to the chops of Sam Presti and Mark Daigneault.

58

THE GLORY

They all went tumbling down: Ja Morant and the Grizzlies, Nikola Jokic and the Nuggets, Anthony Edwards and the Timberwolves, Tyrese Haliburton and the Pacers.

INTRODUCTION

Too Good to Lose and Too Young to Win

June 22, 2025 | Joe Mussatto

Sam Presti sees every season as a chapter in the Thunder's history book.

"What we have this year," the Thunder general manager said days before the 2024-25 season, "is the opportunity to write the 17th chapter, and we're really excited about doing that."

Chapter 17 — spoiler alert — ended with a championship.

The Oklahoma City Thunder claimed the 2025 NBA title, beating the Indiana Pacers in a spectacular seven-game series.

The Thunder was going to be an outlier one way or another depending on how the NBA Finals played out.

On one hand, OKC was too good to lose. A 68-victory regular-season team that seemed destined to raise the Larry O'Brien Trophy. A team that routinely trounced opponents, finishing with the highest average margin of victory in NBA history. A squad defined by its swarming brand of defense.

On the other hand, the Thunder was too young to win. Teams were supposed to fail over and over before they finally broke through. The playoff scars that adorned eventual champions? The Thunder got here with nary a scratch. That's not to say it wasn't earned. Quite the opposite. It spoke to the Thunder's "uncommon" nature, as coach Mark Daigneault liked to say.

The championship was the first in Thunder history. It came 17 years after the franchise relocated from Seattle to Oklahoma City. Thirteen years after its first NBA Finals berth. Nine years after Kevin Durant left Bricktown for The Bay. Six years after the seismic summer of 2019, when the trades of Paul George and franchise icon Russell Westbrook spawned a new era of Thunder basketball.

Shai Gilgeous-Alexander, the prize of the George trade, supplanted Westbrook as the greatest Thunder of them all. SGA, the league's MVP, capped his remarkable season and playoff run with an NBA Finals MVP award.

Jalen Williams and Chet Holmgren rose to the moment, forming a vaunted Big Three alongside Gilgeous-Alexander.

Daigneault, an anonymous name five years ago when he was hired, shepherded the Thunder through it all. After two 20-something-win seasons, the Thunder made the play-in. Then the playoffs as the No. 1 seed. Then, as the No. 1 seed yet again, Daigneault coached the Thunder to the title.

And Presti? Only one line was missing from his resume: NBA champion.

No longer. Hired at 29 as the franchise's general manager, this championship was a culmination of Presti's vision. A vision that became vivid reality

The first 16 chapters of the Thunder built up to an unforgettable 17th: The Championship.

Shai Gilgeous-Alexander blocked a shot from Indiana's Tyrese Haliburton early in Game 7. SGA, the regular-season scoring leader and MVP, was voted the MVP of the NBA Finals after averaging 30.3 points. BRYAN TERRY/THE OKLAHOMAN

HALIBURTON
0
Loves
OKC

THE CHAMPS

BRYAN TERRY/THE OKLAHOMAN

DAYS OF THUNDER

Coach Shuns Limelight after Crowning Moment

June 22, 2025 | Jenni Carlson

Tucked in the far back corner of the temporary stage covered in blue-and-orange confetti, Mark Daigneault positioned himself as far as possible from the action, the interviews, the cameras and the celebration.

Leaning on the railing, he looked as if he could have been observing a November shootaround.

It was an NBA Finals coronation instead.

Make no mistake, the Thunder coach was excited, thrilled, enthused — "I'm just so happy for the guys," he said — and why wouldn't he have all the feels after a 103-91 triumph over the Indiana Pacers in Game 7?

But Daigneault's disappearing act to the back of the stage was telling.

Even with the second-youngest team to win an NBA title, a bunch so young that several of its core players were old enough to drink the celebration champagne Sunday night but wouldn't have been old enough to rent a car Monday morning, Daigneault never treated them like youngsters. He enabled them. He held them accountable. Then, he stepped back and let them become.

What they became was world champions.

"His ability to collaborate with his assistants, then come together and have a clear, concise message for us is second to none," Thunder veteran Alex Caruso said. "He does a great job of pushing buttons when he needs to push buttons. He does a great job of figuring out solutions to problems. Then he does a great job of holding people accountable, which is a huge thing in the NBA."

There were lots of reasons Oklahoma City would spend the next few days celebrating its first world championship. You can start at the top with Clay Bennett and the ownership group, move to Sam Presti and the rest of the front office and then go to Daigneault, the assistants, the support staff and, of course, the players.

But whenever Daigneault was asked how this team got so good so young so fast, he always deferred to the players. Their upbringings. Their backgrounds. Their attitudes.

No doubt all of that was important.

But so was Daigneault's part in this team's ascent.

Take the long view, and you could see Daigneault bringing the Thunder through the early years of its rebuild. Those teams lost a lot of games, but the players who were there say Daigneault never wavered from his core beliefs.

"He always taught me to play the game the right way," defensive Doberman Lu Dort said.

Putting Daigneault with Bennett and Presti, superstar Shai Gilgeous-Alexander said, "They've done an amazing job of building an environment, a winning environment. It's no fluke why we're

Coach Mark Daigneault and Alex Caruso embraced in the closing moments of Game 7 when Kendrich Williams, Ousmane Dieng, Dillon Jones and Ajay Mitchell were dispatched to replace the regulars. CHRISTINE TANNOUS/INDYSTAR

CARUSO
9
55

THUNDER
2

here and why we have so much success and why we've grown so quickly.

"Those guys have done a great job of just giving us a platform to be ourselves and be great, and we did so."

But you could take a shorter view, and see Daigneault's mastery, too.

In these NBA Finals, he went toe-to-toe with Rick Carlisle, a head coaching handful. All that Carlisle did was get the upstart Pacers to the Finals, then despite being an underdog in every game, he figured out a way to push all the right buttons, make one of the most historically great teams in NBA history look pedestrian at times and get to a Game 7.

It was a master class on being a head coach in the NBA.

Even when Indiana's Mr. Basketball, Tyrese Haliburton, went down with an Achilles tear in the first quarter of Game 7, Carlisle and the Pacers managed to keep the game closer for another couple of quarters.

But Daigneault and the Thunder didn't back down.

"One of the great young coaches in all of professional sports," Carlisle called Daigneault after the game.

You would hear no arguments from the Thunder. The players felt Daigneault's influence throughout the playoffs.

"There's a lot of emotions, there's a lot of ups and downs," Dort said. "He's been good at keeping us together. That's the biggest thing; if you want to achieve something like (a championship), we've got to do it together. He did a great job of that."

Thunder newcomer Isaiah Hartenstein said, "He's very stoic in a sense. I think that helped us all ... through the ups and downs in the playoffs. So, I think he's amazing."

But it wasn't just Daigneault's demeanor.

Shai Gilgeous-Alexander scored a game-high 29 points and dished out 12 assists in Game 7. BRYAN TERRY/THE OKLAHOMAN

After Gilgeous-Alexander's poor performance in Game 6, for example, Daigneault was honest with the MVP.

"He told him how he needed to play better," Caruso said. "He was really sticky. He needed to move the ball."

In Game 7, Gilgeous-Alexander dished out 12 assists, a career high in the playoffs, to go with a game-high 29 points. Daigneault demanded better, and Gilgeous-Alexander responded.

"I think that's one of the unique things that Mark brings to the coaching aspect, is just his ability to not really care about ... what the status quo is," Caruso said. "He's going to coach how he knows to coach. It's the same way when he coached me when I was in the G League nine years ago. It's probably the reason he's had the success that he's had.

"He's true to himself."

Even though he was straight-faced during games — "Did he smile tonight when he came to talk to you all?" Caruso quipped — Daigneault was followed and respected and listened to because of the connection that he developed with players. Go back as far as you wanted during his head coaching tenure, and you would find Thunder players who sang praises about their relationship with Daigneault.

From Darius Bazley to Isaiah Hartenstein, the chorus was loud.

"He really cares about us," Hartenstein said. "It's like little details; we bring our kids around, he's the first one to interact with them. If you have any problems off the court, he's always open to talk to you. He's really special, even in the short time, to me."

The admiration was clearly mutual.

Daigneault quipped about the players as they draped towels over his shoulders during his trophy presentation interview after the Western Conference finals. And Sunday as he was interviewed at the end of the Finals, a stack of black championship hats was placed on his head.

He jokingly called them goofy and idiots.

But Daigneault had long realized their greatness, too.

"Everyone says, 'The team is hard to coach,' and usually, that has a negative connotation," Daigneault said. "When you have a team that is this talented, professional, competitive, this willing to sacrifice, that's the ultimate pressure on a coach because you want to serve that. They deserve that.

"But there's no guarantee you end it the way that we did. I just wanted it so bad for them."

And once they had it, Daigneault wanted to step back and soak it in. But he also wanted to step back and let them take center stage because that's what the Thunder coach did this season.

He enabled them to become champions.

"That's what gives me the most pride right now," Daigneault said. "I feel like I was able to do that for them because they deserved all of this." ■

Shai Gilgeous-Alexander was all smiles after adding Finals MVP to his trophy case in addition to his regular-season MVP award. CHRISTINE TANNOUS/INDYSTAR

OKC
OKC

Loves
OKLAHOMA
CITY
8

THE SEASON

NATHAN J. FISH/THE OKLAHOMAN

THE END IS JUST THE BEGINNING

Thunder Enters 2024 Offseason Driven to 'Avoid This Feeling Again'

May 18, 2024 | Joel Lorenzi

Twenty seconds before the final buzzer sounded, the Thunder appeared to be framing a revelatory moment. A stamp for the future instead of an early demise. The Thunder was fighting to extend its season, too concerned with what could unfold next, and yet it seemed as though the play — the one that didn't decide the game — was a suitable freeze-frame for OKC's prologue of a playoff run.

Shai Gilgeous-Alexander in the lane. Chet Holmgren in the air. The star point guard trending toward claustrophobia as four defenders closed in, the promising rookie center extending his crowbar of an arm to flush the incoming lob for a lead.

Everything that led to that point felt appropriately punctuated. Fifty-seven victories. The youngest team to do virtually everything. A refreshing offense, a poised defense. A season of unlikely outcomes for one of the most unlikely No. 1 seeds ever. It fought even to be in position for a Game 7. The lob was the window into possibility.

Then its 2023-24 season ended on the unlikeliest of all outcomes: three free throws.

The Thunder's run ceased with a 117-116 loss to the Dallas Mavericks, ending the Western Conference semifinals in six games. P.J. Washington decided that in a game that featured so much. The spicy words from Luka Doncic to Lu Dort. The rare theatrics from a seemingly relaxed SGA. The boiling feud between Doncic and official Tony Brothers.

Oklahoma City, forced to defend its one-point lead against Doncic with time winding down, saw Doncic back his way down to the block. Dort and SGA each collapsed, leaving the series' first villain, Washington, in his favorite spot — the corner.

By human nature, Gilgeous-Alexander lunged toward him. Washington timed his jumper to align with the body flying toward him. SGA first heard the ball. Then he heard the whistle. Washington, again, would be Dallas' hero. Gilgeous-Alexander's magical playoff stint turned sour.

"I can't look at it," Gilgeous-Alexander said of the replay. "I don't want to look at it. It sucks. You wish you could take the moment back, but it's not the way life works."

Gilgeous-Alexander took ownership of the sequence. He went on about how he shouldn't have fouled, how bitter it was that the season ended by his hand.

Gilgeous-Alexander's connection with Holmgren and the moments leading to OKC's close felt like what viewers would remember. The Thunder only would remember the feeling it felt next.

"It's hard to tell what you remember more, the wins or the losses, but this definitely stings," Holmgren said. "It doesn't feel great. Nobody wins 12 straight championships, so the chances I'm gonna feel this at some point again is definitely there.

"But I'm gonna do everything in my power to avoid this feeling again." ■

Shai Gilgeous-Alexander and the Thunder fell to Luka Doncic (77) and the Mavericks in the 2024 playoffs, which served as motivation heading into the 2024-25 season. KEVIN JAIRAJ/IMAGN IMAGES

OKLAHOMA
CITY
2
MAVS
77

BEST TEAM EVER?

This Thunder Squad Is Built to Clear that Bar in OKC

October 20, 2024 | Joe Mussatto

The 2011-12 Thunder made the NBA Finals, the 2012-13 Thunder was even better, the 2015-16 Thunder was the last great team of a bygone generation and the 2023-24 Thunder was the first great team of a new generation.

As for the best team in Thunder history? You might be looking at it.

The 2024-25 Thunder. Team 17. The one that tipped off this week in Denver.

This may be the finest squad Sam Presti had assembled. And that's saying something. In its 16 seasons of existence, the Thunder had made the playoffs 11 times. The NBA Finals once, the Western Conference finals four times in a six-year span.

"I'm not embarrassed to say we didn't get it done," Presti said in his preseason news conference. "I'm proud to say that we were in the arena; we were in the fight every year. We just got beat sometimes by circumstances and a lot of times just by better teams."

Five times the Thunder finished a season as a top-five team by net rating — point differential per 100 possessions: 2012-13 (9.9 net rating), 2015-16 (7.4), 2023-24 (7.3), 2013-14 (6.4) and 2011-12 (6.3). Four other Thunder teams finished in the top 10 by net rating.

High bar, but this Thunder squad was built to clear it.

"I like the collection of guys that we have," Presti said. "I don't really like to compare the teams because you lose all the context of that point in time."

Presti was right about that.

We forget how good Serge Ibaka and Kevin Martin were on that 2012-13 team, which was derailed in the playoffs when Patrick Beverley crashed into Russell Westbrook. Westbrook, who played all 82 games in the regular season. Kevin Durant, who won the scoring title, played in 81 games.

Just how good is a 9.9 net rating? Only five teams this century had a better net rating: Last season's Celtics. The 2016-17 Warriors, 2015-16 Warriors, 2015-16 Spurs and 2007-08 Celtics.

The argument for the 2024-25 Thunder team to be the best ever was straightforward. It's a year older than the third-best team in Thunder history (by net rating), and it swapped Josh Giddey for Alex Caruso and signed center Isaiah Hartenstein — the franchise's most significant free-agent addition since moving from Seattle to Oklahoma City in 2008.

The Thunder did not have a Terrific Two the caliber of Durant/Westbrook, but it had a perennial MVP contender in Shai Gilgeous-Alexander and a Big Three of SGA/Jalen Williams/Chet Holmgren that rivaled that of Durant/Westbrook/Ibaka.

Gilgeous-Alexander, at 26, was just entering his prime. Jalen Williams was 23, and Holmgren,

Chet Holmgren (7), Shai Gilgeous-Alexander (2), coach Mark Daigneault, Lu Dort (5) and Jalen Williams (8) came into the season determined to make it an unforgettable campaign for Thunder fans. DOUG HOKE/THE OKLAHOMAN

who redshirted as a rookie, was a 22-year-old entering Year 2.

In swapping Caruso for Giddey, the Thunder added shooting and defense. Hartenstein should clean up the Thunder's biggest mess: rebounding.

Lu Dort, the incumbent starter we've yet to mention, was one of the few players who could challenge Caruso as the best perimeter defender in the NBA.

Cason Wallace could defend. Isaiah Joe could shoot. Aaron Wiggins could do no wrong.

Kenrich Williams kept everybody in line. Jaylin Williams kept everybody smiling.

Mark Daigneault, the reigning coach of the year, stayed squinting. And scheming. And quipping. And being outstanding at a job no stranger, no casual NBA fan, even, would peg him for.

This Thunder team had all the goods. The best ever? Until next season, at least. ■

THE ROAD TO 68

A Look Back at a Regular Season that Had It All

Joel Lorenzi

From Shai Gilgeous-Alexander's MVP award, to a 15-game winning streak (that included a loss), to titanic regular-season battles with the Cavaliers, Nuggets and Lakers to 68 victories and to the best point differential in NBA history.

The Thunder's season had it all. Remember when ...

Oct. 24: An opening statement

Thunder 102, Nuggets 87: A year after the Nuggets spoiled the Thunder's 2023 home opener with a 33-point victory, the Thunder returned the favor by hammering the Nuggets on opening night in Denver. Second-year center Chet Holmgren, with 25 points, 14 rebounds, five assists and four blocks, was the best player in a game that featured the reigning MVP (Nikola Jokic, who had 16 points, 13 assists and 12 boards) and MVP runner-up (Shai Gilgeous-Alexander, who had 28 points). Did Holmgren feel stronger after a rigorous offseason? "I would hope so," he said, "because if I'm not, then I did a lot of work for nothing."

Oct. 27: M-V-P! M-V-P! M-V-P!

Thunder 128, Hawks 104: The MVP chants, obligatory by now for Gilgeous-Alexander once in state lines, were far from disingenuous. Despite playing his third game in four nights, SGA mustered the energy for a monstrous fourth quarter in the home opener, erupting for posted 13 points and two assists in eight minutes, spearheading a 13-0 run that erased a one-point deficit and relishing OKC's 39-18 edge over the Hawks in the final period. He finished with 35 points, 11 rebounds, nine assists, three steals and three blocks and shot 11 of 24 from the field and 10 of 11 from the line.

Nov. 6: A blast from the past

Nuggets 124, Thunder 122: In spite of age, altitude and nostalgia, Russell Westbrook punished his former team with 29 points, six rebounds and six assists at Denver. In the closing seconds, Alex Caruso stole the ball from Jokic, but Gilgeous-Alexander's driving layup was blocked by Peyton Watson, ensuring the Thunder's first loss after seven season-opening victories.

Nov. 11: SGA's career high

Thunder 134, Clippers 128: A night after Holmgren suffered a right iliac wing fracture and the Thunder sustained its first home loss (127-116 to Golden State), Gilgeous-Alexander exploded for 45 points, a career high, with nine assists and five steals at Paycom Center.

In the season opener at Denver, Chet Holmgren high-stepped his way to 25 points, 14 rebounds and four blocks. Less than three weeks later, he suffered a fractured pelvis that sidelined him for 39 games. RON CHENOY/IMAGN IMAGES

THUNDER
7
DORT
5
DENVER
15

Nov. 17: An old nemesis

Mavericks 121, Thunder 119: Without centers Holmgren and Isaiah Hartenstein (fractured hand late in the preseason), the Thunder continued to adjust to its tiny times. Despite Luka Doncic out with a knee contusion, the Mavs outrebounded the hosts 54-30. Still, the Thunder nearly avoided its third loss with a late 17-7 run but Lu Dort's flying, dragon kick-looking prayer of a 3-ball missed.

Dec. 10: A statement game

Thunder 118, Mavericks 104: Coach Mark Daigneault downplayed the significance of the NBA Cup quarterfinal. But anyone with a pulse, a memory of last year's I-35 playoff series or even mild curiosity about the blue court knew this was no ordinary Tuesday in December but a rare regular-season statement game. Gilgeous-Alexander scored 39 points. Doncic and Kyrie Irving combined for 33 points. The Thunder outscored the Mavs by 22 points when SGA was on the floor. Doncic, meanwhile, was a minus-14. Plus, Holmgren, owner of the world's largest set of crutches, sat near the bench for the first time since his hip injury.

Dec. 14: Dort's star turn

Thunder 111, Rockets 96: Dort earned his first couple of contracts as a defensive stopper, famed for shutting down a one-man offense like James Harden. In an NBA Cup semifinal at Houston, Dort had a dream night. He blanketed Fred VanVleet, who essentially beat the Thunder two weeks earlier, holding him to eight points on 3-for-15 shooting. Dort also scored 19 points, nailing five of his nine 3-point attempts, and grabbed nine rebounds. "Tonight was a Lu Dort night," SGA said. "Nothing we haven't seen before."

Dec. 17: A loss but not really

Bucks 97, Thunder 81: In a game the Thunder had a chance to win a championship, hoist a trophy and raise a banner — the NBA Cup, but still! — it didn't do much of anything well. Not shooting. Not defending. Not adjusting. Not coaching. "When you lose a game like tonight," Daigneault said in Las Vegas, "it gives you wisdom, it gives you information on yourselves, and as long as we're growing through all those experiences, then we'll gain momentum as the season goes on with still a young team and a team that's growing through everything."

The Thunder scored just 31 points in the second half — only 14 in the decisive third quarter — and shot a dismal 5-for-32 from beyond the arc. Giannis Antetokounmpo posted a triple double: 26 points, 19 rebounds and 10 assists. SGA needed 24 shots for his 21 points, missing seven of his nine 3-point attempts. The only silver lining: The loss didn't count in the standings. The Thunder had won five straight games heading into the Cup final — and then rattled off 10 more victories in a row. After a 105-92 triumph against Boston, the reigning NBA champion, on Jan. 5 at Paycom Center, the Thunder were 30-5, officially owners of a franchise record 15-game winning streak and seven games ahead of Houston in the West and one behind Cleveland in the East.

Jan. 8: Who's really No. 1?

Cavaliers 129, Thunder 122: The battle of No. 1s at Cleveland lived up to the hype: 30 lead changes, SGA's fingerprints everywhere and a furious Thunder offense clashing with a bruising Cavaliers defense. It was the first time in league history that a team on a 15-game winning streak faced a team on a 10-game winning streak. Cleveland's frontcourt proved to be the difference: Jarrett

Cleveland's Evan Mobley and Georges Niag (20) put the squeeze on Isaiah Hartenstein in the season's first meeting between the teams with the league's best records. The Cavaliers won on their court. KEN BLAZE/IMAGN IMAGES

CAVS
20

Allen had 25 points and 11 rebounds, and Evan Mobley had 21 points and 10 rebounds. SGA scored 31 points (although he went 1-for-6 from beyond the arc) and Jalen Williams contributed 25 points and nine assists.

SGA was irked but not distraught: "(We) just lost twice in a month and a half. It sucks that they're the high-profile games. ... Losing twice in a month and a half I'll take, no matter what stage the games are on." SGA also had a message for the national media: "I can't see a world where I'm not in Oklahoma City. Market, no market. I don't care. I love where I am. I'm comfortable where I am. ... I go to work every day with a smile on my face."

Jan. 16: Who's really, really No. 1?

Thunder 134, Cavaliers 114: "The Rematch," they called, though both teams looked unrecognizable. The Thunder didn't have Isaiah Hartenstein because of a calf strain. Cleveland entered with the same crew; its stars were forced to look different. At Paycom Center, the Thunder led by 18 after the first quarter (32-14), by 26 at the half (75-49) and by 38 after the third quarter (119-81). The Thunder even pulled off a 30-2 run. "It felt like seven pit bulls out there," said Cavs coach Kenny Atkinson. "Not five. Seven. ... Their speed and athleticism — they kinda toppled us over."

Mobley scored only five points. Donovan Mitchell, the Cavs' leading scorer, finished 3-for-15 shooting. In the two meetings, he totaled only 19 points while missing 25 of 31 shots. Gilgeous-Alexander scored 40 points with eight assists and might have reached 50 for the first time if he were needed for more than 29 minutes. Still, he leapfrogged Antetokounmpo for the league scoring lead, 31.6 points a game to 31.3.

Jan. 22: Reaching the Big 5-0

Thunder 123, Jazz 114: Fifty was the bane of young Shai Gilgeous-Alexander The Great's early legacy. The lone weapon his detractors could dangle over his head as a scorer. SGA, with more efficiency and consistency and victories than one man needed, never found the reasons to chase it. Until this night at Paycom Center. With just under seven minutes to play, the Jazz trailed by just one, 104-103. SGA put a 23-point first half behind him and scored 18 in the third quarter to enter the fourth with 41 points. He proceeded to score 13 of the Thunder's final 20 points. He amassed 54 points in 37:26, shooting 17-for-35 overall, 3-for-10 from beyond the arc and 17-for-18 at the line. He also had eight rebounds, five assists, three steals and two blocks. "I feel like I wasn't my best tonight, regardless of what the scoreboard says," SGA said. "I could've been better."

Jan. 29: Not really deja vu

Warriors 116, Thunder 109: Just seven days after his first 50-point game, Gilgeous-Alexander dropped 52 at Golden State. But in the locker room, he cupped his hands over his face, his frown unwavering. He sat as dejected as he had been all season. "It sucks," SGA said. "Me, personally, I play to win. Winning comes first. If I don't win, I'm not satisfied. So maybe my 52 points tonight wasn't in the best interest of the team, whatever it is. I'll watch the game over, see where I could've been better."

He entered the fourth quarter with 43 points. He shot a career-high 21 free throws (and made 18). With him on the floor, the Thunder had a 114.5 offensive rating. Without him, OKC had an 82.4 offensive rating.

Shai Gilgeous-Alexander dropped 52 points on the Warriors in a January matchup but suffered a rare loss in a season full of highlights. CARY EDMONDSON/IMAGN IMAGES

Wilson
Loves
OKLAHOMA CITY
2
OKC
GOLDEN STATE
15

Feb. 5: A seven-day itch

Thunder 140, Suns 109: Exactly seven days later, Gilgeous-Alexander struck for 50 again. He had done so three times in his last seven games. "He was cooking," Daigneault said. Only eight other players had scored 50 points three times in such as a short span. Despite SGA's 28 points, the Thunder trailed 63-61 at halftime at Paycom Center. An 13-0 run to open the third quarter turned the tide, and 18 points from SGA produced a 104-79 lead entering the fourth quarter. A baseline jumper with 9:32 left in the game gave him 50 points and the Thunder a 30-point lead at 114-84. A minute later, his night was over. He finished 18-for-29 from the field, 3-for-7 from beyond the arc and 11-for-12 from the line in 34:15. He also had eight rebounds, five assists and two steals.

Feb. 28: What a month!

Thunder 135, Hawks 119: Oklahoma City closed out an 11–2 February that saw its 3-point efficiency skyrocket. Dort sank six threes in the blowout at Atlanta. Through Jan. 1, OKC was the 20th most efficient 3-point team. It finished February shooting 39.1% from deep, second best in the league behind Cleveland (40.7%). In that same span, OKC had the second-best offense with a 124.8 offensive rating. The month's two losses were to Minnesota, 116-101 on Feb. 13 at the Target Center and 131-128 on Feb. 24 at Paycom Center. In between, the Thunder won 130-123 at the Target Center behind 37 points, eight rebounds and eight assists from Gilgeous-Alexander.

March 19: Triple-double backup

Thunder 133, 76ers 100: When Jaylin Williams checked out with 2:09 left in the first quarter, he already had nine points, four rebounds and four assists at Paycom Center. "Triple-double watch," Jalen Williams hollered. The early call was right on point. Jaylin finished with 19 points, 17 rebounds and 11 assists — his second career triple-double, following a 10–11–11 line 12 days earlier against Portland.

March 31: Giddey's return

Thunder 145, Bulls 117: "I had this one circled on my calendar." Those were the words of Josh Giddey, traded to the Bulls over the summer for Caruso. Giddey, a fourth-year guard from Australia, received warm applause when his name was introduced as a starter. "It was fun," he said. "To come back tonight to a nice reception was really special. This is a place I'll hold in my heart forever." He finished with 15 points, 10 assists and eight rebounds in 28 minutes, flashing the potential that attracted general manager Sam Presti years ago.

April 2: Beasts against the East

Thunder 119, Pistons 103: OKC's conquest of the East was complete. Twenty-nine victories. One loss. A .967 winning percentage. The best record against the opposite conference in NBA history. Gilgeous-Alexander scored 33 points, Jalen Williams 23 and Holmgren 22 at Paycom Center. The Thunder's average margin of victory in games against the East was 19.2 points. The only blemish came in January against Cleveland — the only time an East team came within five points of the Thunder. The previous record was 27-3, held by the 1999-2000 Lakers, 2006-07 Mavericks and 2015-16 Warriors. The 1995-96 and 1996-97 Bulls went 25-3 against the West.

Nine months after they were traded for each other, Chicago's Josh Giddey and OKC's Alex Caruso came face-to-face at Paycom Center. Giddey had 15 points and 10 assists; Caruso had seven points. ALONZO ADAMS/IMAGN IMAGES

CHICAGO
3
CARUSO
9

15
NOLA
4

April 6-8: Double dose of Doncic

Lakers 126, Thunder 99 on April 6; Thunder 136, Lakers 120 on April 8: Grudges traveled — maybe even more so than defense — if Doncic's first game against the Thunder as a Laker was any indication. At the beginning of February, the Lakers and Mavericks — with a little help from the Jazz — pulled off the biggest trade in years: Anthony Davis for Luka Doncic. At Paycom Center, Doncic scored 22 points in the first half on April 6. He finished with 30 points in the blowout on 11-for-20 shooting with seven rebounds and five assists. New surroundings, same mastery. "It's very tough to play here," Doncic said. "It brings the competitive spirit out of me."

Two nights later, again at Paycom Center, the teams were in a playoff-like atmosphere when Doncic picked up his second technical foul with 7:40 left in the game. Down by one at the time, the Thunder outscored Los Angeles 29-12 after Doncic's ejection. After sinking a midrange shot for the lead, Doncic looked toward the sideline and used vulgar language. He claimed it was toward OKC superfan Jeremy Price, known as Courtside Tattoo Dude. Price confirmed that he told Doncic his shot was short — and that Doncic responded with an F-bomb. But referee J.T. Orr was standing between Doncic and Price when the incident occurred. According to a pool report with crew chief Tony Brothers, Doncic "looked directly" at Orr, which led to the ejection. "I've never gotten a fan ejected," Doncic said. "But if he's gonna talk, I'm gonna talk back, like always. That had nothing to do with the refs. I didn't really understand." At the time, Doncic had 23 points in 31 minutes on 7-for-15 shooting.

April 9: Home-court advantage

Thunder 125, Suns 112: Just 24 hours removed from a high-intensity victory over the Lakers, OKC gave most of its top rotational players rest on the road. Gilgeous-Alexander, Hartenstein, Dort and Wallace were listed as out with various injuries. That gave Jalen Williams (33 points, seven rebounds, five assists) and Holmgren (22 points, 10 rebounds, 12 of 13 free throws) unique control over the outcome and Phoenix's fate. With its 66th victory, the Thunder secured home-court advantage throughout the playoffs. With their 45th loss, the Suns were eliminated from playoff and play-in contention.

April 13: The best season ever

Thunder 115, Pelicans 100: Game 82 was like so many others: a drubbing. Didn't matter that Gilgeous-Alexander and his best sidekicks were out. Didn't matter that there was nothing to play for. There was, however, history to secure at New Orleans. The Thunder (68-14) increased its average margin of victory to 12.86 points — the best differential in NBA history. The Thunder also became the seventh team to win 68 games. (Golden State owns the record at 73-9 in 2015-16.) "We can appreciate and be grateful for the things we've accomplished and still be hungry," Daigneault said. "Both things can be true." ■

— Justin Martinez, Joe Mussatto and Jenni Carlson contributed.

Even rarely used center Branden Carlson, a rookie out of Utah signed in November, got in on the action with 26 points and 10 rebounds in a season-capping victory over the Pelicans. STEPHEN LEW/IMAGN IMAGES

NBA
MVP
OKC
BYLT
MVP
MVP

BRYAN TERRY/THE OKLAHOMAN

THE TEAM

POINT GUARD

SHAI GILGEOUS-ALEXANDER

Everything is on the Table for the Kid from Hamilton

May 21, 2025 | Joel Lorenzi

Shai Gilgeous-Alexander's eyes darted around the crowd, searching for where he'd begin his speech. There was no script folded into the many pockets embroidered onto his beige button-down.

Rows of white chairs faced his lectern like a ceremony meant for the White House lawn. Dozens more people were scattered around the Thunder's pair of practice courts, the backdrop for SGA's acceptance speech for being voted the NBA's most valuable player.

To his right, Oklahoma City royalty. Clay Bennett, Sam Presti, Mark Daigneault. To his left, his family and team staff. Within arm's reach were his teammates, dressed in shirts with SGA's face and latest feat printed upon them, their wrists blinging with the Rolex watches he had gifted them.

Gilgeous-Alexander scanned over the faces that meant most to him. Then the words came to him. They revealed a side of him, even if briefly, never before seen to the public eye. You have to consider who this was for.

This was for his teammates, he began, who directly impacted his candidacy. A player who averaged 30 points a game for three straight seasons, and yet this was the campaign he managed to help collect 68 victories.

He picked up their dinner tabs, some perhaps as expensive as a Rolex. He stayed in the gym with them. The younger ones, such as Dillon Jones, were fine lugging around Louis Vuitton bags for him. All he did was pour into Jones in return.

They gripped his shoulders when he emotionally plopped back into his seat, embracing him as he sat down for all of 10 seconds between the point he tapped out of his speech and when he realized he had questions to answer.

"You guys are really like my brothers, and I really mean that," Gilgeous-Alexander told them, "and without you guys, none of this would be possible, and I want you guys to know this award is your award, too."

This was for the organization that thought he was worth acquiring. The night he first flew to OKC to complete his physicals, he got shots up. He looked around at Wilson basketballs perfectly fixed on the racks so that the logos faced him. The Gatorade, the towels, all lined up like a Ritz-Carlton.

He was fascinated. SGA considers himself obsessive about the details. When he learned that level of organization wasn't from a janitor with OCD but instead a franchise with it, he knew he belonged.

"I understand the particularness in just making sure everything is right so all you have to do is worry about putting the ball in the hoop or boxing out or rebounding or getting a stop," Gilgeous-Alexander said. "That's what's allowed guys to come here and grow."

Shai Gilgeous-Alexander fulfilled the role as the face of a franchise with championship results. NATHAN J. FISH/THE OKLAHOMAN

Loves
THUNDER
2

This was for "Shai Camp," his crew of childhood best friends and trainers back in Hamilton, Ontario, who helped him work out in the summer. Peculiar — for the superstar to depend on these training methods, and for his friends to dedicate their early mornings to him — but fitting. His physical trainer, Nem Illic, grinned from the front row. His hoop trainer, Nate Mitchell, wasn't in attendance, but surely let his preaching about post-ups rest for one proud night.

This was for his brother, a shade darker than Gilgeous-Alexander but who mirrors him just the same. His father, for starting this journey. His mother, who he called crazy, though he understood her ways all these years later.

"I love the person that she turned me and my brother into," he said.

And then tears flowed. Uncontrollably. He choked up at the mention of his wife, Hailey Summers, who held their son, Ares.

He's branded composure. Packaging his swag in a way the league hasn't quite seen since Allen Iverson, torching teams as a scorer, flashing his thoughts through one-liners. But at this moment, he wasn't too cool.

The nervous laughter had no power over his tears. His wide smile was a faulty mechanism. He felt joy and gratitude so strongly that for the first time, his fans saw him cry. Gilgeous-Alexander wiped his face so firmly he took pores with it, leaving no tear behind.

This was for the family that reshaped his perspective, that matured him in ways basketball couldn't.

"Sorry, I'm so dramatic," SGA said as he tried to fit words in. "Hailey Summers, thank you for everything you are for me, for our son, Ares. You were the first person to show me what love really meant, what sacrifice really meant.

"I wouldn't be the man I am; I wouldn't be the player I am; I wouldn't be the father I am without you. So, thank you for that."

He had been asked on TNT's broadcast by Shaquille O'Neal whether last year's MVP ballot stung him, a landslide of a loss to Denver's Nikola Jokic, who Gilgeous-Alexander bested with 71 first-place votes to 29 this time around. SGA cited the obvious, that it meant more people thought he was undeserving than not.

He wasn't asked again on this day. And while it wasn't his sole source of fuel this season, Gilgeous-Alexander quietly stored last year's results in his mind. Why not him, he wondered.

When he heard the news, SGA thought of each time he was turned away. Each time he was deemed undeserving.

"All the moments I got cut, traded, slighted, overlooked," he said. "I had nights where I thought I wasn't good at basketball, had nights where I thought I was the best player in the world before I was."

This was for him, too. The 26-year-old franchise player, eligible for the richest deal in NBA history. Who laughs at the title of "free throw merchant," who smiled wide at a Denver crowd that taunted him while down in the Western Conference semifinals.

Now, Gilgeous-Alexander was being asked what was left.

"The way I see it," he said, "everything is left. When I picked up a basketball when I was 9 years old, playing AAU, I never sat there like, I want to be an all-star, I want to be an MVP. I sat there like I want to win this tournament."

Gilgeous-Alexander can tap his 9-year-old self on the shoulder. He can pinch the version of him that was cut from junior varsity teams. Splash cold water on the version of him that arrived at Kentucky without a promise to start. The version of him that was told he was letting his NBA youth wither in Oklahoma City.

Everything is on the table for the kid from Hamilton. ■

Shai Gilgeous-Alexander's goal to one day be the MVP was fulfilled during an epic season. During his news conference about the award, he flashed his usual smile but also shed plenty of tears. BRYAN TERRY/THE OKLAHOMAN

KIA
MVP
OKC

BEST OF THE BEST

Ten Games that Defined Gilgeous-Alexander's MVP Season

May 21, 2025 | Justin Martinez

Thunder point guard Shai Gilgeous-Alexander won the NBA's most valuable player award in a runaway.

Out of 100 votes from a panel of sportswriters and sportscasters, Gilgeous-Alexander received 71 first-place and 29 second-place votes. SGA beat Denver's Nikola Jokic, who had 29 first-place and 71 second-place votes. Milwaukee's Gannis Antetokounmpo finished a third.

So how did Gilgeous-Alexander flip the results from 2024's balloting, which saw Jokic crush SGA as the runner-up? Here's a look at the 10 games that defined Gilgeous-Alexander's spectacular season.

10. Beating the Heat

Date: Feb. 12, 2025.
Site: Paycom Center, Oklahoma City.
Score: Thunder 115, Heat 101.
Stats: 32 points (11-22 FG, 4-9 3PT, 6-9 FT), nine assists, five rebounds.
Skinny: Two nights before the All-Star break, the Thunder appeared to have checked out early, falling 21 points behind Miami. But Gilgeous-Alexander woke everybody up by scoring 10 of OKC's first 13 points in the fourth quarter. OKC outscored the Heat 32-8 in the quarter for its largest comeback victory of the season.

9. Topping Luka and LeBron

Date: April 8, 2025.
Site: Paycom Center, Oklahoma City.
Score: Thunder 136, Lakers 120.
Stats: 42 points (14-26 FG, 5-9 3PT, 9-11 FT), six assists, six rebounds.
Skinny: In a star-studded, high-scoring game with LeBron James and Luka Doncic in town, Gilgeous-Alexander turned aside the Tinseltown hype. James scored 28 points and Doncic 23, but the Thunder used a 39-22 fourth quarter for a 16-point victory. SGA had 10 points and two assists playing 7:13 in the final period.

8. This one's for Chet

Date: Nov. 11, 2024.
Site: Paycom Center, Oklahoma City.
Score: Thunder 134, Clippers 128.
Stats: 45 points (13-21 FG, 4-8 3PT, 15-16 FT), nine assists, five steals, three rebounds.
Skinny: In OKC's first game since center Chet Holmgren suffered a fractured pelvis, Gilgeous-Alexander erupted for 45 points, a career high. SGA by the quarter: nine points, 12, 13 and 11.

7. A bigger burden

Date: March 12, 2025.
Site: TD Garden, Boston.
Score: Thunder 118, Celtics 112.
Stats: 34 points (11-20 FG, 2-7 3PT, 10-11 FT), seven assists, five rebounds.
Skinny: It's hard enough to win at Boston. It's even harder to win without one of your All-Star players. But that's what OKC did with Jalen Williams

Shai Gilgeous-Alexander drove to the basket in the third quarter en route to 17 points in that period and 51 points for the game against the Rockets on March 3 at Paycom Center. NATHAN J. FISH/THE OKLAHOMAN

The Official Bank
2
HOUSTON

sidelined by a right hip strain. SGA put the game on ice with two free throws with six seconds left, finishing a 10-for-11 night at the foul line.

6. No panic in Detroit

Date: March 15, 2025.
Site: Little Ceasars Arena, Detroit.
Score: Thunder 113, Pistons 107.
Stats: 48 points (17-26 FG, 4-6 3PT, 10-10 FT), six assists, four rebounds.
Skinny: Remember the victory over the Clippers without Holmgren and the one over the Celtics without Williams? At Detroit, Holmgren and Williams were out. The Thunder started SGA, Cason Wallace, Lu Dort, Isaiah Hartenstein and Kendrich Williams. The Pistons pressed SGA full court during his 38 minutes of action. Asked whether he ever had been more exhausted, SGA replied: "I was very tired. Very, very tired. It's definitely up there." His dagger was two free throws with 13 seconds left, capping a perfect night at the charity stripe. SGA by the quarter: nine points, 11, 17 and 11.

5. MVP showdown

Date: March 9, 2025.
Site: Paycom Center, Oklahoma City.
Score: Thunder 127, Nuggets 103.
Stats: 40 points (15-32 FG, 2-11 3PT, 8-8 FT), eight rebounds, five assists.
Skinny: The scoreboard read OKC vs. Denver — but everyone knew this game was Gilgeous-Alexander vs. Nikola Jokic. In a nationally televised battle between the leading MVP candidates, the combatants were busy: SGA launched 32 shots in 35:25 and The Joke launched 23 in 41:14. Each struggled from beyond the arc, SGA 2 of 11, Joker 2 of 10. They differed at the line: SGA 8 of 8, Joker 2 of 6. Each filled the stat sheet: SGA with eight rebounds, five assists and three blocks, Joker with 13 rebounds, nine assists and three blocks. In the final quarter, the Thunder outscored the Nuggets 41-20. In money time, SGA scored nine points on 4 of 4 shooting with one assist, Joke scored five points on 2 of 2 shooting (but 0 of 2 from the line) with two assists.

4. When 52 isn't enough

Date: Jan. 29, 2025.
Site: Chase Center, San Francisco.
Score: Warriors 116, Thunder 109.
Stats: 52 points (16-29 FG, 2-6 3PT, 18-21 FT), four assists, three rebounds.
Skinny: Despite being one of the league's most unstoppable and consistent scorers, Gilgeous-Alexander had been criticized for never reaching 50 points in a game. He finally did so in January 2025. And the last four games on this list are the four times he hit 50 during the 2024-25 season, when there were only 14 other 50-point games. We start with the one SGA 50-pointer that came in a Thunder loss. Seven days after his first 50-pointer, SGA was distraught in the Bay Area locker room over the defeat. "So maybe my 52 points tonight wasn't in the best interest of the team, whatever it is," he said. SGA by the quarter: 21 points, 10, 12 and nine.

3. Fifty history ...

Date: Feb. 5, 2025.
Site: Paycom Center, Oklahoma City.
Score: Thunder 140, Suns 109.
Stats: 50 points (18-29 FG, 3-7 3PT, 11-12 FT), eight rebounds, five assists.
Skinny: For the third time in his last seven games, Gilgeous-Alexander posted at least 50 points. Only eight other players had scored 50 points three times in such as a short span. The Suns played without Kevin Durant, the former Thunder superstar, and Bradley Beal but led 63-61 at the half. Then SGA posted 18 points in a third quarter the Thunder won 43-16. SGA by the quarter: 13 points, 15, 18 and four (in only 3:39).

Shai Gilgeous-Alexander toyed with guard Isaiah Collier and his Utah teammates as he reached the 50-point mark for the first time in his career. He finished with 54 points on Jan. 22 at Paycom Center. BRYAN TERRY/THE OKLAHOMAN

2. Opening statement

Date: March 3, 2025.
Site: Paycom Center, Oklahoma City.
Score: Thunder 137, Rockets 128.
Stats: 51 points (18-30 FG, 5-9 3PT, 10-10 FT), seven assists, five rebounds.
Skinny: Houston played without Alperen Sengun, Amen Thompson and Dillon Brooks but still put up a fight. Gilgeous-Alexander scored 20 points in the first quarter and 17 in the third quarter as the Thunder carried a 13-point lead into the final period. The Rockets never got closer than six points but couldn't be shaken. SGA by the quarter: 20 points, eight, 17 and six.

1. Barrier broken

Date: Jan. 22, 2025.
Site: Paycom Center, Oklahoma City.
Score: Thunder 123, Jazz 114.
Stats: 54 points (17-35 FG, 3-10 3PT, 17-18 FT), eight rebounds, five assists.
Skinny: A home victory over Utah — *Utah!* — helped boost Gilgeous-Alexander's MVP case? Yes. Because SGA reached the 50-point mark for the first time. And the Thunder needed all of them; Utah trailed by only one point midway through the final quarter. SGA scored 13 of the Thunder's final 20 points. SGA by the quarter: 15 points, eight, 18 and 13. ■

COACH

MARK DAIGNEAULT

As a Kid in Massachusetts, Daigneault Was Destined to Coach

June 3, 2025 | Joe Mussatto

Steve Dubzinski is often asked a variation of the same question: Did you ever see Mark Daigneault becoming this?

The *"this"* part of that prompt has gotten only more unbelievable with time. Did Dubzinski, Daigneault's high school basketball coach in Leominster, Massachusetts, ever see Daigneault becoming an NBA head coach? Coaching in the All-Star Game?? In the NBA Finals???

"I knew he was gonna be successful, and he wanted to coach," Dubzinski said. "Where that journey was going to end? I don't know. Could you have predicted an NBA Finals? Probably not."

Dubzinski was asked The Question by a Boston area TV station recently. And before he knew it, the wisecracking former coach, now a Massachusetts high school sports administrator, had talked himself into an analogy that put Daigneault in rather lofty company.

"I don't think people had Leo in English class as a sophomore and said, 'Oh, that young man's gonna be the pope.' Or Barack Obama in sixth-grade art class and say, 'He's gonna be the president.'"

Dubzinski had to stop himself.

"It's good that I just threw Coach Daigneault in the same category as the president and the pope," Dubzinski said with a laugh.

Daigneault hasn't quite reached world-leader status, but he and the Thunder were four victories from becoming world champs. And back in Daigneault's hometown of Leominster — 1,700 miles from Oklahoma City — that's a pretty big deal.

The Daigneault family is beloved in the town of 44,000 just west of Boston. It's Celtics country but given the Thunder's ties to the area with Daigneault, general manager Sam Presti and assistant GM Rob Hennigan, there's a proud pocket of Thunder orange and blue in the Bay State.

Daigneault is an old soul. Anybody who has known him will confirm. It's as true of Daigneault at age 40 as it was when he was 14.

"Perfect way to put it," said Billy McEvoy, who met Daigneault in the fourth grade. "He would take a ribbing from his group of friends for that."

"Let loose," they would tell Daigneault.

But Daigneault, even as a kid, was always the adult in the room.

"He was the captain of our high school basketball team for the qualities you look for in a captain — he was a leader, he led by example,"

Coach Mark Daigneault had proven to be the perfect young coach to grow with the young Thunder franchise.
NATHAN J. FISH/THE OKLAHOMAN

OKC

McEvoy said. "Not even just in sports. I have kids now, and you want your kids to be friends with someone like Mark Daigneault."

Dubzinski described Daigneault as a "cerebral" player who "got the most out of his athletic ability."

In other words, a good high school basketball player who maybe could have played small-college ball, but who was destined to coach.

Daigneault was a shooter, "make no mistake about it," Dubzinski said. And a charge-taker that would make Jaylin Williams proud.

"I'm not surprised they're as good as they are defensively because Mark defended," Dubzinski said. "He was the master at taking the charge. It was before the flop, so maybe that played a little bit into it, frankly. But he could sell it."

Daigneault leads the No. 1 defense in the NBA — a juggernaut of a unit that's hardwired for freneticism. The Thunder's offense is buoyed by the league's MVP, Shai Gilgeous-Alexander, whose coolness is contrasted by Daigneault's *everymaness.*

"He hasn't changed who he is as a person despite the enormous success that he's had," McEvoy said. "I love that about him."

After five years as head coach of the Oklahoma City Blue in the G League and one season as a Thunder assistant under Billy Donovan — one of Daigneault's many mentors — Daigneault was elevated to Thunder head coach prior to the 2020-21 season.

Having navigated the Thunder through its rebuild with a development-first approach, the implementer of Presti's plan, Daigneault is now leading the most dominant squad in basketball. The Thunder set an NBA record for average margin of victory en route to a 68-victory season.

Now Daigneault, in Year 5, is opposite Rick Carlisle, dean of the college of coaches, in the NBA Finals.

"He's been very good to me as I've come up here," Daigneault said. "Couldn't have more respect for him."

No one is questioning the coaching chops on either sideline, but Daigneault's team is stocked with more talent. OKC was an overwhelming favorite to win the title and raise the franchise's first title banner since relocating to the plains in 2008.

"It's obviously a great opportunity for all of us," Daigneault said. "Everybody that gets to participate in the NBA Finals, it's something to be grateful for. And one of the cool things is you get to share it with the people you care about and the people that care about you."

Like the people who knew Mark Daigneault back in his Leominster days, when they knew what he wanted to be, but not how far it would take him.

"He was born," McEvoy said, "to be a coach." ■

Mark Daigneault and the Thunder posed in the bright lights of media day prior to the season with goals of playing under the brighter lights of the 2025 NBA Finals. DOUG HOKE/THE OKLAHOMAN

OKC

SMALL FORWARD

JALEN WILLIAMS

From Overlooked Prospect to NBA All-Star: That's the Jalen Williams Way

June 4, 2025 | Justin Martinez

The road that serves as the entrance to Perry High School in Gilbert, Arizona, soon will receive a name change.

Jalen Williams Way.

It's the school's way of celebrating one of its most notable alums.

Williams has received plenty of accolades throughout his rise to stardom, but this one might be the most fitting. It symbolizes a player who has paved his path, going from overlooked in high school to squarely in the spotlight on basketball's biggest stage.

"It's really cool," Williams said. "They kind of made me the player that I am today as far as understanding the game, how to approach the game and how to watch film. They introduced me to a lot of that, so I'm always thankful for that. ... It's really like a full-circle moment to have something that's gonna stay at school."

SPROUTING IN THE DESERT

After becoming the head coach at Perry, Sam Duane Jr. held an open gym in the summer of 2016. Among those who showed up was Williams. Duane had never seen the soon-to-be sophomore play, so he initially marked him down for the junior varsity team.

It was a natural assumption. Williams was a self-described "5-8, 100-pounds-soaking-wet kid" in a state that rarely received rain. And his body hadn't yet grown into his dangling arms, which he could practically jump rope with.

But none of that stopped Williams from tearing up the competition that day. He made up for his lack of size with knockdown shooting over taller opponents, and he made up for his lack of athleticism with sound fundamentals.

He was taught them at a young age by his parents, Ron and Nicole, who had Division I basketball aspirations before they joined the Air Force.

"I could tell he was skilled," Duane said. "I could also see that he really had a high IQ for the game. He played with no fear, just like he does now. That was my first impression of Jalen."

Williams made the varsity and wasted no time becoming a contributor as a sophomore.

College programs weren't as quick to notice. An exception was Santa Clara, which stumbled upon the young guard in July 2017. He was playing in an AAU tournament at American Sports Center in Anaheim, California. The 242,000-square-foot building was the country's largest indoor wood-court facility at the time, making the thin-framed

The rapid improvement of Jalen Williams in just three years in the NBA had been essential in Oklahoma City's rise to perennial contender status. NATHAN J. FISH/THE OKLAHOMAN

Love's
THUNDER
8
OKC

Williams a needle in a haystack.

It didn't help that he was playing in the back corner of the complex, either. He might as well have been in the deserts of Arizona, as few college scouts ventured that far from the watering hole of talent on the center stage.

But Williams' AAU coach, Paul Suber, managed to flag down Santa Clara assistant Jason Ludwig. And Williams was on the Broncos' radar once Ludwig watched him play. Santa Clara sent someone to most of Williams' AAU games after that. This included coach Herb Sendek, who had an eye for talent. He coached another Thunder great, James Harden, at Arizona State from 2007-09.

"We kept a close eye on (Williams) and really followed him," Sendek said. "He had a beautiful-looking stroke. And at the same time, you could tell when looking at him that his body wasn't finished yet."

Williams sprouted to 6-feet-3 by his senior year, and he was able to dunk finally. He averaged more than 25 points a game and led Perry to the 6A state semifinals.

Williams received offers from programs such as Hofstra and UC Santa Barbara. But after years of building a relationship with its staff, the unranked guard committed to Santa Clara.

BLOSSOMING WITH THE BRONCOS

As soon as the door swung open, Josip Vrankic knew Williams was different. He was on a visit to Santa Clara in early 2018. And Vrankic, a sophomore forward, joined the Broncos' staff in taking the recruit to lunch.

The first thing Vrankic noticed when Williams stepped out of the car was his pair of trendy white glasses. The second thing he noticed was that Sendek, usually a reserved person, was also wearing a pair as a joke.

"They called them 'drip glasses,'" Vrankic said with a chuckle. "I was like, 'Coach is wearing them for this kid?' I was in shock. Coach Herb never — I don't want to say goes out of the comfort zone — goofs around like that, especially with a new recruit."

Chalk it up to Williams' personality, which was infectious once he arrived on campus.

He was — and is — still a kid at heart. His college room was decorated with Marvel's Avengers action figures and youth backpacks, like one of Lightning McQueen from "Cars." And he proudly sported a lunch box of "Pinky and the Brain," one of his favorite TV shows growing up, that he got from a flea market.

Williams also wore a smile at each practice as if it was part of his uniform. And he had so much bounce in his step that he made the basketballs look as if they needed more air.

"He's an every-day guy," Sendek said. "I've met very few people like him in terms of how he may have a bad moment, but I've never seen him have a bad day. It just never seemed to me that work was drudgery for him. Even now, he plays with a spark of joy, and that's how he was with us."

He became Santa Clara's best perimeter defender as a freshman. Williams averaged a team-high 1.3 steals and cracked the starting lineup in his 11th outing. He never lost that spot.

Williams also hit another growth spurt during his freshman season. He was now 6-6, which gave him a size advantage over his opponents, and he still retained the guard skills he learned throughout the years.

Santa Clara began to run its offense through Williams more often during his sophomore season. By the time he was a junior, opposing teams had no way of matching up with him. Williams earned an All-West Coast Conference first-team selection with career-high averages of 18 points, 4.4 rebounds and 4.2 assists.

"He was able to do everything," Vrankic said. "You didn't know who to put on him. If you put a smaller guy on him, he's bigger and he shoots over you. If you put a bigger guy on him, he drives by you. He also had the ability to pass, rebound and defend. It was like a perfect blend of opportunity and timing."

OKC's Big Three of Jalen Williams (with his trademark towel), Chet Holmgren and Shai Gilgeous-Alexander chatted with ESPN's Lisa Salters after winning Game 4 in the Western Conference finals. JESSE JOHNSON/IMAGN IMAGES

When Williams declared for the 2022 draft, OKC selected him with the 12th pick. After earning an All-Rookie first-team selection in 2023, he continued to develop into one of the league's best two-way players.

RETURNING TO HIS ROOTS

Williams' diamond chains shimmered with every microscopic movement as he fielded questions after OKC eliminated Minnesota in the Western Conference finals. He couldn't stop shining if he wanted to.

That's Williams' life these days. The guy many college scouts placed a low ceiling on has become a household name. He's an All-Star with All-Defensive second-team and All-NBA third-team selections under his Chrome Hearts belt. And he swapped out his "Pinky and the Brain" lunch box for a player-exclusive pair of Adidas Harden Vol. 9 sneakers with the show's colors.

Williams received all of that this season, only his third in the NBA.

He regularly returns to Gilbert in the offseason, and those at Perry High gladly open the gym doors when he does. Once Williams enters, he still has the same hunger of that high school kid who craved a hoops career. And he still has the same lighthearted approach that now counters the weight of stardom.

It's the Jalen Williams way. ■

7

CENTER

CHET HOLMGREN

Losing Young Big Man Was Tough; So Was Bringing Him Back

June 4, 2025 | Jenni Carlson

Chet Holmgren adopted a routine this past winter that he never wanted to repeat.

After an in-game fall fractured his hip in six places, he was confined to bed for weeks. That's the only way bone can fuse back together, and while the Thunder big man knew his body was healing, his psyche was hurting.

"I'd wake up, go on my phone, eat, and then I would take a super long nap," he said. "Then I'd wake up and do that again, then I'd go back to sleep."

He paused as if rewinding those dark days.

"And I had to do that until I could walk," he said, "so it was brutal."

So brutal that the self-proclaimed hoops junkie had to avoid basketball. Oh, he'd go onto YouTube and watch mash-ups and pull-ups.

"But live games," he said, "I had to take a step back for a couple of weeks."

He said he wasn't in a good headspace. Why did something he loved so much keep breaking him? Why had his dedication led him back to the injured list less than two years after a foot injury erased what would have been his rookie season?

Watching his team or, well, any team play was like peroxide on a sidewalk-scraped knee.

Only six months later, Holmgren, 23, wasn't just back on his feet. He's walking down Nikola Jokic and Ruby Gobert. He's a big reason the Thunder reached the NBA Finals. His rim-protecting defense. His floor-spreading offense.

He had been masterful in these playoffs, actually upping his numbers in the postseason.

Regular season: 15.0 points on 49.0% shooting and 8.0 rebounds.

Playoffs before the finals: 16.4 points on 49.2% shooting and 8.6 rebounds.

"He's always been a very self-driven, self-motivated, hard-working player," Thunder guard Aaron Wiggins said. "Before injury, after injury, still the same work ethic and same approach. But I definitely do think ... there's probably just a sense of gratefulness and appreciation to be healthy and have that opportunity to do the thing that we love."

Watch Holmgren play now, and it's easy to forget how recently he was bedridden — and how brilliantly he came back from that.

The injury happened on Nov. 10 against the Warriors. As Holmgren patrolled the paint, Andrew Wiggins made a hard drive down the baseline toward the basket. Holmgren rose with

Instead of flexing his newfound muscle, Chet Holmgren played in only 32 regular-season games. The Thunder, though, was able to integrate him back into the rotation in time for the playoffs. BRYAN TERRY/THE OKLAHOMAN

Loves
THUNDER
7
OKC
OKC

Wiggins, but near the top of his jump, his left leg kicked out and gravity took over. The wiry 7-footer landed hard on his right hip.

Holmgren's face immediately contorted as trainers rushed to his side. The way one of them draped a towel behind Holmgren's head so people watching in the arena and on TV wouldn't be able to see his face was telling.

It was bad. Doctors and X-rays confirmed it; Holmgren had a right iliac wing fracture.

Basically, a broken pelvis.

Oklahoma City had been without Holmgren before when a torn Lisfranc ligament in his right foot forced him out of the entire 2022-23 season. But the injury, which occurred during a pro-am game, and the resulting surgery happened in August, so the Thunder knew well before the season began that he wouldn't be available.

What happened in November was different.

"This was a particularly tricky one," coach Mark Daigneault acknowledged, "because he's such a high-impact player and we were having such a great season."

The Thunder had started by winning eight of its first nine games, and as well as it was playing, Holmgren was matching that excellence. He had four games of 20-plus points and four games of 10-plus rebounds.

His averages: 18.2 points, 9.2 rebounds, 2.9 blocks.

Losing him was tough on the Thunder. So was bringing him back.

Or it should've been. When Holmgren returned to the lineup on Feb. 7 against the Raptors, he had missed 39 games and been sidelined for almost three months. He was going to need time to ramp up.

But he was trying to jump on a moving bullet train. The Thunder had won 40 games, opening up a six-game lead in the Western Conference and establishing itself as the favorite to take the top seed.

"Him integrating back in was a challenge and could have tripped a wire," Daigneault said. "And it didn't."

While he gave credit to the rest of the players — "the team did a great job of allowing that process to take place without judgment and just let it unfold and grow over time," he said — Daigneault and others gave the biggest share of praise to Holmgren.

"He was a professional the whole time," guard Isaiah Joe said. "He knew that he wanted to come back and pretty much be right where he left off whenever he touched down back on the court with us. So, he did a really good job on his off hours, taking care of his body, trying to get in the best shape that he can.

"And ... he stayed present. He stayed present in practices and all that. He had asked questions and just tried to stay up to speed so whenever he came back, he wasn't really missing any beats."

Holmgren didn't play 30-plus minutes a game right away. He didn't play more than three consecutive games until the final two weeks of the season, either.

But in his first game back, he had four blocks. In his second, five. A week and a half later, he scored 20 points, followed in his next game with an 8-for-11 shooting performance.

Daigneault thinks all of that was the seed for what bloomed in these playoffs.

"As well as we were playing then," he said, "I think we're more complete now and certainly have a higher ceiling as a team now in terms of how we can play and the impact we can have."

Chet Holmgren shook off the rust from his game with perseverance and then he polished the Oscar Robertson Trophy with his new T-shirt after the Thunder won the Western Conference finals. BRYAN TERRY/THE OKLAHOMAN

Joe said, "It was kind of like he never left, at least for us anyway."

Holmgren remembers things a bit differently.

"Every time I think about it ... the thing that pops into my mind is it was (expective) up," he said.

Hard to argue.

Holmgren has endured two major injuries that cost him nearly half of his three seasons in the NBA. That kept him from the game he loves. That left him unable to get around without crutches when he wasn't confined to bed.

Nowadays, he tries to put all of that out of his mind. And yet as he talks, it is clear that his embrace of the present is influenced by the difficulties of his past.

"If anybody can say it's not guaranteed, it's me," he said. "Just understanding that anything can happen, so you've just got to go out there and give it your all leading up to it, give it your all in games and really just enjoy it.

"Because it's not guaranteed." ■

GENERAL MANAGER

SAM PRESTI

In 2019, Executive of Year Prophesied 'the Rise of Another Great Team'

June 5, 2025 | Joe Mussatto

"Given the events of the last few weeks, I think it is important for all of us who love the Thunder to reflect on where we have been, where we are now, and most importantly where we are going — as well as how we plan to get there."

That's how Thunder general manager Sam Presti opened his op-ed, "Looking back, thinking forward," published in The Oklahoman on July 25, 2019.

Presti, the Thunder's architect, revealed in it his blueprint for the Thunder's rebuild in transparent detail. Words penned more than 2,000 days ago that now, with the NBA Finals tipping off in Oklahoma City, read as prophetic.

Presti wrote the op-ed in between phone calls with Houston general manager Daryl Morey. In the Thunder's practice facility on the night of July 11, 2019, Presti finalized a trade sending franchise icon Russell Westbrook to the Rockets. Also in the practice gym that night was Shai Gilgeous-Alexander, who had just arrived from Los Angeles as part of the Paul George trade.

"If this guy ever becomes a player," Presti thought, "I've got to remember this story."

SGA became the MVP, a scoring savant. Jalen Williams, a pick from the Clippers that the Thunder aced, became an All-Star and All-NBA player. Chet Holmgren, the embodiment of lottery luck after a 24-victory season, is destined for All-NBA teams if he stays healthy.

Together they form a homegrown Big Three. Gilgeous-Alexander is the oldest, a month shy of 27. Williams and Holmgren recently turned 24 and 23. The comparisons to Kevin Durant, Westbrook and James Harden are irresistible. Thirteen years separate their respective NBA Finals runs, with Presti as the throughline.

The Thunder, rather than making a hasty trade to accelerate the process, looked forward to a time when the primes of Gilgeous-Alexander, Williams and Holmgren would overlap. And here the Thunder is, in the NBA Finals, with two-thirds of its Big Three still in the pre-prime of their careers.

The rest of the league might shutter at the thought, but the Thunder's era of overlapping primes is still in the distance.

Back to Presti's op-ed.

"In saying goodbye to the past," he wrote six years ago, "we have begun to chart our future. The next great Thunder team is out there somewhere, but it will take time to seize and discipline to ultimately sustain."

The next great Thunder team arrived sooner than anybody, Presti included, reasonably could have expected. In 2025, Gilgeous-Alexander topped

General manager Sam Presti preached patience as he rebuilt OKC after trading Paul George and Russell Westbrook and later enduring 22- and 24-win seasons. The big payoff came with an NBA title. BRYAN TERRY/THE OKLAHOMAN

Denver's Nikola Jokic and Milwaukee's Giannis Antetokounmpo for the league's most valuable player award. Also in 2025, Presti beat Cleveland's Koby Altman and Detroit's Trajan Langdon for the league's executive of the year award.

OKC, counting the playoffs, was 80-18 heading into the NBA Finals against the Indiana Pacers.

The Thunder won a combined 46 games in the 2020-21 and 2021-22 seasons.

Even then, there were "very early flickers," Thunder coach Mark Daigneault said of OKC's potential.

The rebuild worked because Presti hired a coach willing to implement it with a superstar who was aligned in executing it.

"He was honest and upfront with me from Day 1," Gilgeous-Alexander said of Presti. "I think that helped our relationship right away. You don't get that very often, especially that early."

There was mutual understanding between Presti and SGA.

"Nothing more than just two guys with good character trusting each other and having one common goal in mind."

A common goal that has been six years in the making.

Just as Presti prophesied.

"The people of Oklahoma City should be able to one day watch the rise of another great team," Presti closed his op-ed, "as they have watched the rise of their rebuilt downtown, with the knowledge that they are witnessing something not only great, but enduring ..." ■

Shai Gilgeous-Alexander and Sam Presti chatted in the presence of the Oscar Robertson Trophy (given to the Western finals champion) and the Magic Johnson Trophy (given to SGA as the series MVP). BRYAN TERRY/THE OKLAHOMAN

Finals
2025
NBA
CHAMPIONS
OKC

MANUFACTURED IN THE USA
BALON BLASTER
HOMELAND
paycom center
OKC

NATHAN J. FISH/THE OKLAHOMAN

THE GLORY

WESTERN CONFERENCE FIRST ROUND

THUNDER 131 | GRIZZLIES 80

GAME 1 • APRIL 20, 2025 • OKLAHOMA CITY

A RECORD ROUT

Thunder Puts the Grisly in Grizzlies

Joe Mussatto

Shai Gilgeous-Alexander was out of sorts.

After missing eight of his first nine shots, Gilgeous-Alexander drained a 3-pointer just before halftime. He raised his arms toward the Paycom Center rafters — a gesture that screamed "finally!"

Part of SGA's charm is not taking himself too seriously. He wasn't close to his best in the Thunder's playoff opener, but he wasn't frustrated. And given the result, why would he be?

The Thunder took Game 1 from the Grizzlies by 51 points: a 131-80 Easter Sunday shellacking.

We knew this Thunder team was scary good, but how it won Game 1 was spine-chilling. Soul-crushing. Laughable, but only if you're into gallows humor.

In a playoff game in which OKC won by half a hundred, SGA scored a season-low 15 points. This is the NBA scoring champ we're talking about. A guy who waltzes his way to 20 points without a misstep. A dud scoring night from a superstar would sink most normal teams. Even good normal teams.

But this Thunder squad happened to be otherworldly. Game 1 was yet another reminder.

"That's what a team is," coach Mark Daigneault said. "You don't want to be dependent on one player for anything. Lu Dort's a great defender, but our defense shouldn't be predicated on how Lu defends. That's what teams do, is they pick each other up. They compensate each other."

Of course the most dominant regular-season team in NBA history would open the playoffs with one of the most dominant postseason victories we've ever seen — the largest margin of victory in a Game 1 in NBA history.

OKC led by as many as 56 points. When the Thunder had 83 points, the Grizzlies had 38. Even into the second half, the Grizzlies had more turnovers than field goals. Aaron Wiggins, who logged zero minutes in the first quarter, led the Thunder in scoring with 21 points. Alex Caruso was a plus-30 without attempting a shot. OKC went on a 23-2 run to open the second quarter, and that was without Gilgeous-Alexander. That's no slight to SGA, but more so evidence of the Thunder's depth.

Gilgeous-Alexander averaged 36.3 points on 54% shooting against the Grizzlies in the regular season. He led the Thunder in scoring in the four matchups with Memphis, all OKC victories. That's what made his 4-for-13 clunker in Game 1 all the more surprising. The Grizzlies are not equipped (who is?) to guard him. Rookie Jaylen Wells would have been assigned to SGA, but Wells was out with injury. Scotty Pippen Jr. tried his best to wrangle Shai, but Pippen Jr. was seven inches shorter than Pippen Sr. That's a problem.

SGA got to his spots. His shots just didn't fall.

"The goal (today) when we woke up was to win the game," SGA said, "and nothing else mattered. We did that. Whatever it looks like, I'll take it." ■

Chet Holmgren helped dominate Desmond Bane and the Grizzlies in a Game 1 blowout with 19 points and 10 rebounds in only 21 minutes of action. He went 3-for-4 from beyond the 3-point arc. SARAH PHIPPS/THE OKLAHOMAN

WESTERN CONFERENCE FIRST ROUND

THUNDER 118 | GRIZZLIES 99

GAME 2 • APRIL 22, 2025 • OKLAHOMA CITY

BEAR DOWN

Thunder vs. Grizzlies Hardly Rates as a Fair Fight

Joe Mussatto

Shai Gilgeous-Alexander whipped the ball behind his head to Lu Dort, who was standing alone at the top of the arc. Dort canned the 3-pointer.

It was then that commissioner Adam Silver should have intervened. Such ridiculousness shouldn't fly in a playoff game. The referees should've waved the game off. The league should've called the series then and there. The Grizzlies were down without a whimper, and the Thunder kept throwing haymakers.

The good news for Memphis? It improved by 32 points from Games 1 to 2. The bad news for Memphis? The Grizzlies still lost Game 2 by 19 points, 118-99.

We've now seen two blowouts. Do we really need to watch two more of these?

"Don't get it backwards," Thunder coach Mark Daigneault said. "We were ready for them to play really well tonight. We knew that wasn't who they were Sunday. There was a fatigue element to that. ... Down 2-0, they're going back home in front of their home crowd where they play well. The last time they played there they played excellent, so we've gotta be ready for a similar type of punch in Game 3."

Anything short of a sweep would be surprising. Forget figuring out Memphis' path to win the series. What could the Grizzlies do to win a game?

Game 2 wasn't nearly as ugly as Game 1, but they mirrored each other in some ways.

The Thunder blitzed Memphis from the opening tip and built a huge first-quarter lead. Gilgeous-Alexander wasn't efficient — he's shooting 33% for the series — but it hadn't mattered. (He still scored 27 points.) Ja Morant was a mess for most of the game. Jalen Williams and Chet Holmgren outplayed Desmond Bane and Jaren Jackson Jr. The Thunder's depth shined and the Grizzlies' lack of it was glaring.

Think the Grizzlies could use Kenrich Williams? He can't get on the floor for the Thunder. Aaron Wiggins, the Thunder's leading scorer in Game 1, scored eight points in seven minutes in Game 2. Wiggins was the Thunder's ninth man. He'd be the sixth man for Memphis.

The Grizzlies showed fight in the second half, outscoring the Thunder by seven points in the third quarter. It's the one quarter Memphis has won through the first two games.

"We understood that they were gonna come out aggressive, playing free," Holmgren said. "We had to match that, counter that. We didn't come out lacking any intensity."

Really, though, the game was won in the first quarter. OKC outscored Memphis 32-17. The Thunder played like the more desperate team, which went against human nature. You'd figure the team that lost Game 1 by 51 points would show some urgency.

"Coach does a lot of philosophical teaching to us throughout the season," Holmgren said. "Whether we won or lost by however many points you pick, it's gonna be the same mindset coming in." ■

Shai Gilgeous-Alexander and the Thunder continued to pummel the Grizzlies in Game 2 with a 19-point victory. Gilgeous-Alexander had 27 points, eight rebounds and five assists. BRYAN TERRY/THE OKLAHOMAN

WESTERN CONFERENCE FIRST ROUND

THUNDER 114 | GRIZZLIES 108

GAME 3 • APRIL 24, 2025 • MEMPHIS

A TALE OF TWO HALVES

Thunder Rallies from 29 Points Down to Take 3-0 Series Lead

Joe Mussatto

Thunder-Grizzlies Game 3 was unlike all the rest. And by all the rest, I mean every other Thunder game we've seen this season. Eighty-two regular-season games, one NBA Cup final and two playoff games ... none of 'em followed the twists and turns of Game 3 at Memphis.

The Thunder beat the Grizzlies 114-108, erasing a 29-point deficit to take a 3-0 lead in their first-round series.

And as these playoffs plod along, this was one we might look back on. Not because the Thunder won, but because of how the Thunder won.

Most of OKC's victories had a similar shape. No team in NBA history had more double-digit victories or a higher margin of victory than the Thunder. Only twice did OKC trail by 29 or more points prior to Game 3. The Thunder's largest comeback victory was 21 points in a February home game against the Heat.

The Thunder, by virtue of all of those blowouts, played the fewest clutch-time games. A concern heading into the playoffs? I guess, but what was the Thunder supposed to do, strategically try to win by slimmer margins?

You can't manufacture pressure. Can't simulate situations like the Thunder faced at the FedExForum.

First, a mea culpa. I'm the moron who joked after Game 2 that Adam Silver should call off the series. That Thunder-Grizzlies wasn't a fair fight.

Well, it didn't look like a fair fight in the first half of Game 3.

The Grizzlies smacked the Thunder around for two quarters. The Thunder looked discombobulated and, worse, disinterested. Memphis' "others" were otherworldly. Scotty Pippen Jr. and Santi Aldama outscored Shai Gilgeous-Alexander and Jalen Williams in the first quarter.

Memphis kept cruising until a sudden crash. Lu Dort, unintentionally, it seemed, undercut Ja Morant in midair on a fast break just before halftime. Morant fell hard on his hip. At the time of his exit, the Grizzlies led by 27 points.

After scoring 77 points in the first half, the Morant-less Grizzlies managed just 31 points in the second half.

Chet Holmgren's 3-point shooting and Alex Caruso's hustle sparked the comeback. Holmgren made four 3-pointers in the third quarter (and he finished with 24 points). Caruso made 40 winning plays, at least it felt like it, in the fourth quarter alone.

SGA remained out of sorts — shooting sub-40% for the third time in three games — but Williams starred as a second option. On the road, no less. SGA scored 31 points, Williams 26.

The big what-if from Game 3 was Morant. What if he didn't land hard on his hip? The Grizzlies almost certainly win the game. While Morant's exit swung the door open for a comeback, it didn't cheapen OKC's effort. It didn't stop a young OKC squad from banking a new experience.

You have to win in different ways in the playoffs, and this Thunder victory was unlike any other. ■

The Grizzlies made Shai Gilgeous-Alexander and the Thunder work for the win, but they managed to overcome a 29-point deficit to take a 3-0 series lead. STU BOYD II/THE COMMERCIAL APPEAL

WESTERN CONFERENCE FIRST ROUND

THUNDER 117 | GRIZZLIES 115

GAME 4 • APRIL 26, 2025 • MEMPHIS

SEIZE THE MOMENT

Regular-Season SGA Returns to Complete First-Round Sweep

Joel Lorenzi

Shai Gilgeous-Alexander answered questions this week that he often hadn't all season.

About his comfortability. His shotmaking. What he saw that viewers didn't. Any and everything that could hope to explain a three-game stretch that, in terms of efficiency, didn't appear to match the MVP finalist's standards.

In the dwindling seconds of Game 4, with a sweep on the line, he ripped those questions from the tips of every naysaying tongue, sinking a midrange silencer just shy of the 3-point line that left Kevin Garnett smiling somewhere. A 23-foot, six-inch reminder of who he was.

By his hand, the Thunder swept the first round of the NBA playoffs for a second consecutive season, deflecting Desmond Bane's intentionally missed free throw in the final second of a 117-115 Game 4 victory to bat away Memphis' chances at a Game 5. Gilgeous-Alexander played into all his MVP, game-closing, midrange-loving ways.

That included the dagger, which gave the Thunder a five-point lead with 11.6 seconds remaining. And a step-back 3 deep into the fourth quarter to give OKC a double-digit lead — one it quickly squandered to a feisty Grizzlies team sans Ja Morant — a shot that hadn't always been kind to Gilgeous-Alexander through four games. Both punctuated a 38-point performance on 13-for-24 shooting, complete with five boards and six assists.

The Thunder, bloodthirsty and seemingly equipped with eight hands per player, bought Gilgeous-Alexander some time in the series to return to the efficiency that had become standard.

In Game 4, OKC forced 22 turnovers, turning those into 32 points. The Thunder closed with 94 shot attempts, 14 more than the Grizzlies. More opportunities with the ball meant more chances for Gilgeous-Alexander to probe his way to his kill spots, dancing to find his rhythm again.

He started the night with an immaculate first quarter, 16 points on 7-for-7 shooting. After just a single shot in the second quarter, he posted 19 points in the second half, connecting on looks he had yearned to hit for a series. The elbow jumpers he held so near and dear to his heart. The incredible high-glass finishes that fit his crafty ways.

Chet Holmgren (11 points, four blocks) wondered about the questions he received about Gilgeous-Alexander. He saw his point guard swiftly weave between defenders for four games. Holmgren watched him rise up over double teams for a signature jumper that had been unbeatable for the better part of 82 games. He saw the ingredients of the MVP finalist he had known, just without as many makes.

Holmgren's tone bordered on dismissive when

Jalen Williams helped the Thunder cruise to a 4-0 series sweep with 23 points, four rebounds and five assists.
PETRE THOMAS/IMAGN IMAGES

asked about the progression of SGA's series.

"I don't know where this 'ups and downs' thing is coming from," Holmgren said. "I thought he played a hell of a series. I felt like he was out there making the right reads.

"It's an imperfect game. Shai's never gonna go 25-for-25 in a game — I hope he does, but probably not. He was making the right plays all series, trusting people. That's been really helpful, not only for myself, but for (Jalen Williams), everybody down the list. I don't see that changing."

Gilgeous-Alexander, in his second playoff run as the Thunder's franchise player, claimed he learned nothing about himself in the series.

"I'm impressed with my (ability) to stay with it," he said. "In the past, I for sure would've turned down the aggressiveness a little bit. I made a jump as far as that this year. That's something I'm definitely proud of. In the past, I would've shied away from the moment because of where my shooting was headed." ■

WESTERN CONFERENCE SEMIFINALS

NUGGETS 121 | THUNDER 119

GAME 1 • MAY 5, 2025 • OKLAHOMA CITY

SQUANDERED

Holmgren's Misses at the Line Lead to First Playoff Loss

Joel Lorenzi

The last image of Chet Holmgren came with his fingers laced atop his head, his arms held there in shock from the moment the shot fell to his escape down Oklahoma City's tunnel and out of sight.

Astonishment locked his limbs in place. Of all the ways Game 1 of the Western Conference semifinals could have played out, the sequence most cruel to him was what viewers likely would remember. What he'll remember.

A pair of botched free throws with 9.5 seconds left with the Thunder up by one point. Holmgren's long pauses, his cheeks puffing with exhalation and the stress of a smoker on his face between each miss. The blink of a trip down for the Nuggets and Aaron Gordon, who drilled the game-winning 3-pointer over Holmgren's outstretched arm.

Six seconds changed his and the Thunder's fate.

"I have to be better," Holmgren said after a stunning 121-119 loss. "I'm not one to shy from accountability. I have to be better. I have to execute better, especially down the stretch. We worked too hard as a collective, and we're too far along in this thing for situations like that to happen."

That the Thunder's firm grip could be stripped so quickly left Holmgren frozen. A 14-point lead in a game that saw OKC leading by 11 with less than five minutes to play, its first action in nine days. Squandered.

Oklahoma City's offense ran into a wall — and Nikola Jokic's stout chest — in the few minutes prior. With 4:31 to play, Shai Gilgeous-Alexander — tethered to Jokic by the MVP race — drilled a step-back 3 with Gordon nearby and Christian Braun underneath him for an 11-point lead, 113-102. SGA finished with 33 points, 10 rebounds and eight assists on 12-for-26 shooting.

The Thunder scored two field goals the rest of the way: An Isaiah Hartenstein push shot with just over three minutes to play and an SGA dunk on a sidelines-out-of-bounds play with 11.1 seconds remaining.

For much of the second half, Jokic teetered on the fence of his sixth and final foul. All the while, Thunder coach Mark Daigneault alternated between Holmgren and Hartenstein, each of whom collected five fouls, in an effort to avoid the dreadful fate of facing Jokic with just one of the two.

Even the two weren't enough. Eighteen of Jokic's 42 points came in the fourth quarter, connecting on eight of his 10 free-throw attempts in the period. For the night, he also had 22 rebounds and six assists.

Before Holmgren felt the weight of the world on his bony shoulders, in a game shaved down to a single possession for the final 1:14, the Thunder repeatedly fouled the Nuggets while up three. It meant that Holmgren needed to make both foul shots to best evade an upset.

Holmgren shrugged at the idea that Denver's championship mettle played a role in its comeback. ■

Despite Shai Gilgeous-Alexander's 33 points, 10 rebounds and eight assists, the Thunder suffered their first loss of the playoffs in Game 1 against the Nuggets. SARAH PHIPPS/THE OKLAHOMAN

WESTERN CONFERENCE SEMIFINALS

THUNDER 149 | NUGGETS 106

GAME 2 • MAY 7, 2025 • OKLAHOMA CITY

'WE KNEW WHAT WAS AT STAKE'

OKC Evens the Score with Record-Setting 87-Point First Half

Joe Mussatto

The 60-victory club has been under siege this second round.

The 64-victory Cavaliers are down 0-2 to the Pacers.

The 61-victory Celtics are down 0-2 to the Knicks.

In NBA history, home teams that trail 0-2 in a series have gone on to lose the series 88% of the time.

Gulp.

It was under that ominous backdrop that the 68-victory Thunder, down 0-1 to the Nuggets, tipped off at Paycom Center in Oklahoma City.

The Thunder, in what became clear from the jump, had no interest in sharing company with the beleaguered beasts of the East.

"We knew what was at stake tonight," point guard Shai Gilgeous-Alexander said.

Oklahoma City pummeled Denver 149-106, making sure the demons from Game 1 were denied entry to Game 2. The Thunder scored 87 points in the first half — an NBA playoff record. OKC led Denver by as many as 49 points. Gilgeous-Alexander was a plus-51 in his 30 minutes — the best plus/minus in a playoff game. Ever.

"Winning by 100 or winning by two, it's still 1-1," Gilgeous-Alexander said.

He's right, of course. Denver did its job. It earned the all-important split, stealing home-court advantage as the series headed to the Rockies. Doesn't matter that OKC was a plus-41 through two games.

But don't you know Boston or Cleveland would love to trade places with OKC?

Before the Thunder's victory, the home team in these NBA playoffs had lost seven games in a row.

"It's definitely on your mind no matter what, but regardless of what has happened, we have to worry about what we can control going forward," Gilgeous-Alexander said.

OKC broke the curse and then some.

SGA was brilliant. He scored 34 points on 13 shots. He was 11-for-11 from the foul line. He had eight assists against two turnovers. Compare that to Boston's Jayson Tatum, who was 5-for-19 in the Celtics' Game 2 collapse against the Knicks.

Nikola Jokic outplayed SGA in Game 1. That flipped in Game 2.

The Thunder limited Jokic to 17 points, eight rebounds and six assists — as pedestrian of a stat line as you'll ever see from the big Serbian. Jokic was a minus-36 to SGA's plus-51.

Including SGA, eight Thunder players scored double-digit points: Jalen Willimas (17), Chet Holmgren (15), Isaiah Hartenstein (14), Isaiah Joe (14), Aaron Wiggins (10) and Ajay Mitchell (10).

Gilgeous-Alexander wasn't about to let the Thunder lose. What happened to the Celtics and Cavs wasn't for him.

"At the end of the day, you never know what a series is gonna look like," Gilgeous-Alexander said. "You just have to worry about the next game and be better for the next game. Wherever it takes you, it takes you."

Takes the Thunder to Denver, all tied up. ■

Shai Gilgeous-Alexander soared for a dunk over the Nuggets' Peyton Watson. Gilgeous-Alexander was one of eight Thunder players who scored double-digit points in Game 2. SARAH PHIPPS/THE OKLAHOMAN

WESTERN CONFERENCE SEMIFINALS

NUGGETS 113 | THUNDER 104 (OT)

GAME 3 • MAY 9, 2025 • DENVER

'NOTHING'S WRITTEN'

Gilgeous-Alexander Musters a Smile While Denver Fans Jeer

Joel Lorenzi

Shai Gilgeous-Alexander peered into the crowd during his stroll off the court and smiled, the only visible set of teeth amid a line of seething Thunder players.

Jeers swelled in his direction. His ears perked up at them, as if he had pressed his head against a phone call with his detractors. If he wasn't already aware, the white sea in Denver made note of his admitted deplorable Game 3 performance on his way off the floor.

A missed opportunity. A typically buttery scorer watched a fourth quarter slip through his hands.

Nuggets star Nikola Jokic was fortunate to escape — "basically, I was the worst player on the court today," he said — walking the halls of Ball Arena in a suit that looked to be an ode to his namesake (The Joker), an eggplant jacket with an emerald vest. And yet it was Gilgeous-Alexander who chuckled as he walked away from the rubble.

"Some fans were taunting me," Gilgeous-Alexander said after the Thunder's 113-104 Game 3 overtime loss. "And I know how the game goes. I know how life is. It's easy to taunt when you're up, and I don't ever want to show them that I'm defeated or mad or anything like that.

"Nothing's written. The series is not over."

Oklahoma City, down 2-1 in these Western Conference semifinals, had seen the series swing by a mere handful of possessions. Gilgeous-Alexander was reminded of the ones he had a hand in.

He entered the fourth quarter with 8:31 left, a one-possession game in OKC's favor. With 5:19 to play, he launched an unsuccessful leaning 3 in a tight window. The next possession was a 22-foot 2-pointer with little separation. Just over a minute later, SGA fired off another step-back 3. Front rim. Two possessions later, Gilgeous-Alexander missed that exact shot.

Gilgeous-Alexander finished with 18 points on 7-for-22 shooting (31.8%), his second-most inefficient performance of these past two postseasons; only his 4-for-13 showing in a series-opening victory against versus Memphis was worse.

He went 1-for-8 in the fourth quarter and didn't attempt a shot in overtime. According to ESPN, 18 of his 22 attempts were contested. His teammates shot just 7 of 24 (3-for-11 from deep) on his passes.

"A few of those shots felt good," SGA said. "More than a few. It ultimately felt like a lot of settling for jumpers. ... The way I see it, you live or die by your decisions. Tonight, I died by my decisions."

The Thunder were outscored 22-19 in the fourth quarter and 11-2 in overtime.

Jalen Williams had 26 of his 32 points, as well as 10 of his 16 fourth-quarter points, by the time Gilgeous-Alexander rejoined the Thunder on the court in the final quarter. Williams took just two shots in the last 8:31 of regulation.

Williams minimized it: "We have the best closer in the NBA." ■

Oklahoma City stumbled to down 2-1 in the series against Denver as Shai Gilgeous-Alexander struggled from the floor, shooting just 7 of 22 for 18 points. RON CHENOY/IMAGN IMAGES

WESTERN CONFERENCE SEMIFINALS

THUNDER 92 | NUGGETS 87

GAME 4 • MAY 11, 2025 • DENVER

NEXT MEN UP

A Big Three from the Bench Prevents a 3-1 Deficit

Joe Mussatto

The Thunder's Big Three came through.

Alex Caruso, Aaron Wiggins and Cason Wallace, that is.

Give each of them a game ball because without the opportunistic play of the three benchmen, this was a 3-to-1, all-but-over series. Instead, it's a 2-2 split heading back to Oklahoma City after the Thunder won 92-87 in Game 4.

Wiggins was a team-best plus-14 in his 16 minutes. Caruso and Wallace, who played 28 and 23 minutes respectively, were a plus-12. Those were the three best plus-minus marks for the Thunder. Single game plus-minuses can be deceptive, but nothing about those numbers was a fluke.

After an overtime period in Game 3 and a quick turnaround ahead of Game 4, "we made a very intentional effort to use our depth today and get everybody going," Thunder coach Mark Daigneault said.

OKC's biggest advantage over Denver was its depth. In Game 4, the Thunder's bench outscored the Nuggets' bench 35-8.

In a game where 3-pointers were precious, Caruso, Wiggins and Wallace accounted for eight of the Thunder's 10 long-range makes. Combined, they shot 8 of 14 (57%) from 3. The rest of their teammates were 2 of 27 (7%).

The triples from that bench trio were timely, too. Down six points midway through the third quarter, Wiggins buried a 3, assisted by Wallace, to cut Denver's lead in half.

Down six later in the third quarter, Wallace made a 3-pointer to cut Denver's lead to three yet again. On OKC's next possession, Wiggins drilled another 3.

Wallace, with 10:43 left in the game, hit a 3 to narrow Denver's lead to four points. Wallace then hit his third 3 — on as many attempts — to give the Thunder a two-point lead with 8:35 to play.

Caruso's 3-pointers (he was 2 of 5) came earlier in the game, but he was as clutch as could be in the fourth quarter. Doing classic Caruso things, like punching the ball out of Nikola Jokic's hands for a Thunder rebound and junking up Denver's offense by applying relentless pressure.

"They were huge," Daigneault said of his bench. "They made huge shots, and they gave us huge defense and toughness plays in that stretch of the game. Big, big time."

Caruso played all but seven seconds of the fourth quarter. Daigneault rode Caruso in place of starter Lu Dort, who wasn't used at all in the quarter. Caruso didn't make a shot in the quarter, but he was instrumental in the Thunder outscoring the Nuggets 29-18 in the final frame.

Shai Gilgeous-Alexander brought the game home with nine points in the fourth quarter and a team-high 25 overall, but he didn't get much offensive help from his main sidekicks. Jalen Williams played excellent defense but had to beg for a bucket. Same goes for Chet Holmgren. Combined, J-Dub and Chet shot 6 of 23, including 0 of 8 from 3-point range. ■

Aaron Wiggins was part of a big bench effort for OKC in the Game 4 victory with 11 points and six rebounds in 15:46.
ISAIAH J. DOWNING/IMAGN IMAGES

WESTERN CONFERENCE SEMIFINALS

THUNDER 112 | NUGGETS 105

GAME 5 • MAY 13, 2025 • OKLAHOMA CITY

'IT'S ABOUT TIME'

SGA Delivers in the Clutch in Epic Duel with Jokic

Joel Lorenzi

His expression was flat, the visage of expectation.

After the shot, after the victory. That Shai Gilgeous-Alexander rose up so freely in the biggest game of his life — among the most weighted games in Paycom Center's history — was not lost on him. He had said all series that he was befitting of the moment.

It called for him to not just push the Thunder past Denver in a 112-105 victory for a 3-2 series lead, but to do it with the shots that had betrayed him for several games. With a look that gnawed at him. Challenged him. Threatened his playoff legacy.

A pull-up 3 with 47.7 precious seconds left, uncontested so as to acknowledge his relationship with the shot. SGA trotted down the court without eruption, without twisting his face. The temperament of someone who thought they had been deserving.

Gilgeous-Alexander didn't just meet the moment. His name tag was fastened. He enunciated. He shook its hand with a vice grip that would make Adrian Peterson wince.

"It felt like," Gilgeous-Alexander said of his late jumper, pausing to find the words, "like it's about time."

Fate asked Gilgeous-Alexander and his Thunder to come back from a nine-point deficit — which felt more like 18 — with nine minutes left. To throw hands with an all-timer, a near-300 pound star who swung his heaviest hand of the series; Nikola Jokic made 17 of his 25 shots, missed just two of his seven 3-point attempts, and logged 44 points and 15 rebounds.

OKC endured. It left the ring with bloody knuckles. What did Thunder birth certificates say again?

Their finishes in Games 1 and 3 evoked conversations of whether their adolescence held them back in the spotlight. An X-ray of Game 4 showed signs of the team that emerged in the fourth quarter, a squad that could close a game at all costs.

The non-Jokic Nuggets core shot just 1-for-15 in the final quarter. Denver went scoreless for roughly six minutes. So, Jokic asked SGA to dance. They tangoed in one of the most memorable superstar duels in recent memory.

Twenty of SGA's 31 points came in the second half on 8-for-12 shooting. Jokic scored 25 in the same half. Gilgeous-Alexander created 15 straight points. Jokic scored 11 straight. The big man ambled into floaters. The slim one zipped down the lane, floating backward into jumpers.

With less than two minutes left, Jokic widened the human imagination. From 27 feet out, he used one foot to launch a Sombor Shuffle heave over Chet Holmgren's reach to tie the game at 103.

"I think it was really easy for us to probably cave in a couple times," Jalen Williams said.

Instead, Williams (18 points, nine rebounds) drilled the most monumental 3 of his career. Then SGA nailed his pull-up 3 for a six-point lead, grabbed the defensive rebound and made two free throws for a game-sealing 111-103 advantage. ■

While Denver superstar Nikola Jokic dropped 44 points and 15 rebounds, Shai Gilgeous-Alexander's 31 points, six rebounds and seven assists were just enough to give the Thunder the pivotal Game 5 victory. BRYAN TERRY/THE OKLAHOMAN

WESTERN CONFERENCE SEMIFINALS

NUGGETS 119 | THUNDER 107

GAME 6 • MAY 15, 2025 • DENVER

GROWING PAINS

Williams' Seesaw Series Bottom Outs at a Bad Time

Joe Mussatto

Jalen Williams, a towel draped atop his head, sat alone on the Thunder's bench as his teammates trudged across the court. Williams stared up at the scoreboard: Nuggets 119, Thunder 107.

Who knows how long Williams might have sat there had Alex Caruso not helped him up. Upon standing, Williams pulled the towel tighter.

For Williams, the towel was so often a victory prop. In Game 6, it veiled defeat.

Williams scored six points in the loss. He shot 3-for-16 from the floor. He missed all four of his 3-point attempts.

"I think I had a good process with what I was doing," he said. "I just hurt us tonight (by) not making shots."

Whether Williams could emerge as a true No. 2 scoring option was a lingering question heading into these playoffs. The answer depended on the game. And that's the problem.

For the Thunder to win Game 7, for it to go all the way, OKC needed more consistent play out of its second All-Star. Williams' bad games — bad shooting games, at least — outnumbered his good ones in these Western Conference semifinals.

He was tremendous in the Thunder's Game 3 overtime loss, scoring 32 points on 52% shooting. And he was good in the Thunder's Game 2 rout. In the other four games, however, he had shot 15-for-63 (24%). For the series, he was 7-for-33 (21%) from 3-point range.

At times, he looked like a just-turned 24-year-old in his third NBA season and fourth playoff series. Like a guy dealing with a nagging wrist injury that may or not be affecting his play. Failure often was a prerequisite to playoff success.

That's the conundrum with J-Dub and the Thunder. In the regular season, he was so good, this team was so good, that we started to move the goalposts. They hit all the historical benchmarks of being a championship team — and they might very well snatch the Larry 'O in a few weeks. But history also told us they were too young, too inexperienced. No matter its fate, the Thunder would be an outlier one way or another.

Williams had become a symbol of that seesaw. It was an oversimplification to say the Thunder would go as far as he went ... but the Thunder might go as far as he goes. Shai Gilgeous-Alexander couldn't do it all, and Chet Holmgren — who might be the second-best player — wasn't ready to be its second-best option.

SGA scored 32 points on 69% shooting. He was only slowed by foul trouble. Williams, on this night as much as any, had an opportunity to not just shine alongside SGA, but in the absence of him. It didn't happen.

"It's life, it's basketball," Gilgeous-Alexander said. "Tonight wasn't his night, clearly. The best part about it all is he has an opportunity to change all that. If he has a big game next game, nobody remembers, nobody cares." ■

Jalen Williams had another off night in the Game 6 loss, scoring only six points on 3 of 16 shooting from the floor. Nikola Jokic's 6-foot-11, 284-pound presence didn't help matters. ISAIAH J. DOWNING/IMAGN IMAGES

WESTERN CONFERENCE SEMIFINALS

THUNDER 125 | NUGGETS 93

GAME 7 • MAY 18, 2025 • OKLAHOMA CITY

J-DUB'S REVENGE

Williams Redeems Himself as Thunder Finally Eliminates Denver

Joe Mussatto

Jalen Williams barely slept on the eve of Game 7.

"I was just excited to play," he said. "You never know how many Game 7s you're gonna get, and it's an opportunity to be great."

Would Williams be great? Good, even?

Game 6 ended on that cliffhanger. A scene of a distraught J-Dub that left everybody wondering whether the Thunder's second star would show up in the Game 7 finale.

Spoiler alert: He did.

Williams redeemed himself and then some in the Thunder's 125-93 close-out rout of the Nuggets.

He was the best player in the biggest quarter of the season — the second quarter of Game 7, a period the Thunder won 39-20. A quarter in which the Thunder had as many steals (six) as the Nuggets had field goals.

"He brought his A-game when we needed it most," Shai Gilgeous-Alexander said of Williams, "and that's what makes you the upper echelon in this league."

Williams, a first-time All-Star, kept pace all by himself with the Nuggets in that second quarter. He scored 17 of his 24 points. He shot 8 of 11 in the frame and was 10 of 17 for the game.

Along with his 24 points, Williams had a team-high seven assists against one turnover. He grabbed five rebounds and made one steal.

"Great force, especially early," Thunder coach Mark Daigneault. "It was definitely a conscious effort by him to use his speed and his power. He was on the gas from the jump tonight."

Williams and the Thunder took full advantage of a hobbled Aaron Gordon, who gutted out Game 7 through a hamstring strain. Gordon, to his credit, grabbed 11 rebounds. But he was a step slow defensively. And without a full-go Gordon, the Nuggets' defense was leaky.

It was death by a million backdoor cuts.

Williams and the Thunder pounded the Nuggets in the paint, outscoring Denver 64-42.

The ghost of playoff past — yes, just one of them — followed Williams this postseason. Williams shrank in the Dallas series a year ago, but then again, he was a second-year player asked to be the No. 2 option in the second round of the playoffs.

That was the same ask of Williams in these playoffs, now as a 24-year-old with another season of experience on his resume.

His results were inconsistent in this series, but bouncing back from a Game 6 clunker with a clutch Game 7 showed maturity from a player who didn't always have that (see above: he's 24).

Jalen Williams bounced back in a big way in Game 7 against the Nuggets with 24 points, five rebounds and seven assists in 32:41. He finished a plus-35, tops among the starters. SARAH PHIPPS/THE OKLAHOMAN

Loves
THUNDER
8

"You talk about bouncing back, no player in the playoffs in this competitive of a series plays great every night," Daigneault said. "(Nikola) Jokic is as good as anybody, obviously — he didn't play great every night in the series.

"It's hard. Dub, I think because he's in his third year, takes a little more flak for that, but it's hard to perform in the playoffs. ... But he rises up every time. He did last year in the Dallas series. Game 6 was his best game after some struggles, and tonight was his best game after some struggles as well."

Jokic managed only 20 points in Game 7, going 5-for-9 from the field, 1-for-2 from beyond the arc and 9-for-11 from the line. Gilgeous-Alexander posted 35 points on 12-for-19 shooting with four assists, three steals and zero turnovers.

On the postgame podium, Gilgeous-Alexander sat next to Williams.

How did SGA think Williams played?

"Terrible," Gilgeous-Alexander said in jest.

"Nah, he was amazing," SGA continued. "Dub was a big reason for our little stretch of the lead in the second quarter. Gave us momentum. His growth as a basketball player, we've seen it all year, but his growth mentally has been more impressive to me. He wouldn't have played the way he played today last year, and I know that 100%.

"To see him take that step forward, it's a really proud moment for me. Just knowing what he goes through on a day-to-day basis, knowing where he comes from, like that's really my brother."

As Gilgeous-Alexander kept answering questions, Williams yawned.

He was due for some good sleep. ■

Alex Caruso played a key role off the bench in dispatching the Nuggets in Game 7, adding 11 points, three assists and three steals. SARAH PHIPPS/THE OKLAHOMAN

COMMITMENT RUNS

WESTERN CONFERENCE FINALS

THUNDER 114 | TIMBERWOLVES 88

GAME 1 • MAY 20, 2025 • OKLAHOMA CITY

SETTING THE TONE

Kenrich Williams' 'Invisible Work' for Thunder Pays Off

Jenni Carlson

Walking to the scorer's table with the opening game of the Western Conference finals still in the first quarter, Kenrich Williams marveled.

"Man, these are real minutes," he thought. "I haven't got to play in the playoffs yet, and my number's being called in the Western Conference finals."

Then, he got the chills.

"Just extremely grateful," he said.

Williams wasn't the only grateful one. On a night the Thunder came out sluggish — hard to find fault in that after a Game 7 just two days ago — it got a shot in the arm from Kenny Hustle. A kick in the butt, too. He changed the tone of the game. Or perhaps he set it in the Thunder's 114-88 victory.

"Our energy was not where it needed to be in the first whatever amount of that game," coach Mark Daigneault said, "and he changed it."

Williams was an unexpected sub in the first quarter. Well, actually, he'd have been unexpected had he checked in at any point with the game in the balance. After all, he didn't play a single meaningful minute in the seven-game series against the Nuggets.

Not one.

"Well, first of all, he hasn't played significant minutes since the last game of the regular season, which was five weeks ago," Daigneault said. "The amount of invisible work that it takes to keep yourself that sharp to be able to go into a playoff game like that, a Western Conference finals, and perform the way he did, the invisible work shows up there. That unbelievable consistency, professionalism, mental toughness, all that stuff."

When Williams checked in, the Thunder found itself down 20-17. Not terrible, but not exactly a rousing start. But Williams immediately cranked up the physicality. Within the first few seconds he was on the court, he went after a rebound, and even though he didn't snag it, he found a Timberwolf and got a body into him. The Thunder forced a turnover on a shot-clock violation later in that possession.

While Williams' minutes at the end of the first quarter didn't do much to change the scoreboard — the Thunder trailed by three when he checked in and still trailed by three at the end of the quarter — his play resonated with his teammates.

"I watch K show up every single day, regardless of the situation or what's going on in the games," center Chet Holmgren said. "He shows up, and he makes things happen. When I see somebody doing that, I know that they're always ready."

Seeing Williams play hard energized the guys around him. They knew that he didn't play with any of the games hanging in the balance in the Memphis series. Ditto for the Denver series. They knew, too, that he could have hung his head. Sulked. Stewed. Grumped. Griped.

Seldom-used Kenrich Williams, alias Kenny Hustle, didn't even play 10 minutes, but he left his mark on Game 1 as a plus-19 with nine points on 3-for-3 shooting and three rebounds. SARAH PHIPPS/THE OKLAHOMAN

Instead, Williams stayed fully engaged. When Holmgren missed free throws at the end of Game 2 and left the door open for the Nuggets to make a game-winner, Williams was the one who nursed the big man's psyche back to health. When young Thunders who didn't play much meet for games — they're called the "high-intensity guys" — Williams is always there.

"We've been playing basically every game day or every other game day," he said. "Just keeping me sharp. Letting me stay in shape. Very competitive."

When he returned to action in the third quarter, he immediately grabbed a defensive rebound. Then the next time down the floor, he snagged another one. It helped spur the Thunder to a 10-0 run.

He finished with eight points on 3-of-3 shooting, making the two 3-pointers he attempted. He grabbed three rebounds and was a plus-19 despite playing only 9:36. ■

WESTERN CONFERENCE FINALS

THUNDER 118 | TIMBERWOLVES 103

GAME 2 • MAY 22, 2025 • OKLAHOMA CITY

UNDER THEIR SKIN

Thunder's 'Intensity and Aggressiveness' Wearing Down Timberwolves

Joel Lorenzi

Jaden McDaniels' fourth-quarter flagrant foul hardly required a body language specialist. Two hands and a thrust was a shove, the universal sign for frustration — the most telling league-wide symptom that the Thunder defense had seeped into the bloodstream.

Other symptoms included but were not limited to: hands flailing or shoulders shrugging in the direction of referee Scott Foster, seeing six heads instead of the three-headed snake that OKC's Big Three was in Game 2, a 118-103 Thunder victory.

Through two games, the toxicity of the Thunder's defense had bubbled. Third quarters had come strapped in, delivered by lethal injection. The runs, crushing when they happened, felt inevitable for OKC, even so deep into these playoffs.

They knew it. They weaponized it.

"Our intensity and aggressiveness can wear on you," guard Alex Caruso said. "Whether you're physically aware of it or mentally aware of it. By the time we bring in our second unit, first unit's already pushing. And then you bring in me, Cason (Wallace), and keep one of the bigs out there. It's like you have a whole new starting five defensively."

The margin of error in this series was seemingly as small as it had ever been against this Thunder squad. Game 2's third-quarter run was 25-6, in a quarter with all the same furiously forced turnovers. Nothing tipped the building over quite like Wallace's lob to Chet Holmgren, who leaped as if he swung from a branch in order to extend his frame and slam it home.

Of all the things that the Timberwolves' odds were hinged on, very little was swinging their way. Minnesota was meant to outrebound the Thunder; OKC's 14-12 edge in second-chance points wasn't helpful. Not an exemplary ball control team entering the series, its best bet was to inch closer to the median; the Thunder led the points-off-turnovers count 52-20 this series.

Minnesota digested the Game 1 film and seemingly set out to force the Thunder into more jumpers. OKC attempted 12 more 3s (making just 27.3% of them) and notably depended on an abundance of midrange jumpers.

MVP Shai Gilgeous-Alexander lived there, fully licensed. Jalen Williams had similar credentials, though he bordered on audacious in Game 2. He was 10-for-14 on 2-pointers. The wrist snapped in all the right ways en route to 26 points, 10 rebounds and five assists.

Between the barrage of jumpers, OKC still managed to torment Minnesota on the interior: 22 more points on 2s, and 16 more points in the paint on 69% shooting.

OKC had outscored Minnesota by 28 points in the third quarters. Even when Minnesota threatened Game 2's 24-point lead, trimming it to 10 in the fourth quarter, the Thunder budged about as far as Foster would on a coach's challenge.

"I don't know if we get the due credit we deserve for how we've learned and how we've grown as a team," Caruso said. ■

Lu Dort and the OKC defense made Minnesota superstar Anthony Edwards work for his 32 points, as he went 12 of 26 from the floor, including 1 of 9 from deep. NATHAN J. FISH/THE OKLAHOMAN

WESTERN CONFERENCE FINALS

TIMBERWOLVES 143 | THUNDER 101

GAME 3 • MAY 24, 2025 • MINNEAPOLIS

OUT OF CHARACTER

Back on Home Turf, Minnesota Brings the Fight

Joel Lorenzi

The Thunder probably didn't need a film session for the realization. It scarfed down the leftovers of Game 3 anyway, confirmation of what it felt like in real time.

Those who spoke on behalf of Oklahoma City seemed to come to a common conclusion. The team that suited up against Minnesota in Game 3's143-101 loss wasn't the team that won 68 regular-season games.

"Yeah, I think we just played a little out of character," guard Alex Caruso said.

Minnesota outscored OKC 34-14 in the first quarter and 38-27 in the second for a 31-point halftime lead.

The expressions and look of the Thunder was unlike what it had shown. The loss of the turnover battle, its first of this postseason. The loss of power in the paint, the first of its kind this series.

"It was obvious that we didn't play the way we usually play," guard Cason Wallace said. "They got to the rim, they got passes, like they had whatever they wanted. They were the more aggressive team.

"We didn't have the fight for it."

The Timberwolves brought the fight, though. It was evident in the way forward Julius Randle (24 points) shoved his way to position on box outs and on the wing. In the way star Anthony Edwards (30 points) forced his way down to the lane, down the throats of the OKC defense.

That it happened at the expense of the Thunder's will, with the Timberwolves being the aggressors, was the surprise. The turnovers that OKC forced through two games, which drove the Wolves crazy, left the Thunder well empty.

Turnovers, despite the Thunder not focusing on them, had been a catalyst. For the season and this series. Wallace didn't seem convinced that Game 3 was more than an anomaly.

He also expressed confidence that, should OKC return to its identity, turnovers wouldn't be the only way it could win.

"We haven't been in that situation many times," Wallace said. "But throughout the game, like (if) we're playing to our standard and doing the things that we usually do, (if we) don't win one section, we'll win another."

Regardless of whether the Thunder felt Game 3 could be replicated or not, that it happened still left a sour taste. The Thunder surely seemed more confident than any team with a playoff loss of such magnitude.

"It's a loss, no matter how much we lose by," Wallace said. "But watching film, seeing the way that we lost, definitely gives us an edge for tomorrow."

Caruso added: "Looking forward to having the opportunity to go out there and be who we are, rather than let them dictate terms their way." ■

Naz Reid (11) and Mike Conley (10) made things hard on Isaiah Hartenstein and the Thunder, handing them a rare blowout loss as the series shifted to Minneapolis for Game 3. BRUCE KLUCKHOHN/IMAGN IMAGES

WESTERN CONFERENCE FINALS

THUNDER 128 | TIMBERWOLVES 126

GAME 4 • MAY 26, 2025 • MINNEAPOLIS

FAMILY AFFAIR

Cousins Gilgeous-Alexander and Alexander-Walker Fill the Stat Sheet

Joe Mussatto

A diamond-framed sports card holder hung from a chain around Vaughn Alexander's neck.

Inside were two trading cards. One Shai Gilgeous-Alexander card, one Nickiel Alexander-Walker. Each depicted in his Team Canada jersey. Either was visible depending on how the chain was flipped. Sometimes it was SGA's turn to be forward facing. Other times, Nickeil got the shine.

And that's exactly how Game 4 went, Gilgeous-Alexander and Alexander-Walker taking heroic turns in a Western Conference finals bout that doubled as a one-on-one, cousin vs. cousin duel.

"I'm just so proud of both of them," Vaughn Alexander, SGA's dad, said after the Thunder's 128-126 victory.

Gilgeous-Alexander dropped a game-high 40 points. Alexander-Walker had 23 to lead the Timberwolves. The MVP vs. Minnesota's man off the bench.

"He got the better of me sometimes, I got the better of him," SGA said. "Stuff we've dreamt about for our whole lives, and it's crazy that it's come to fruition."

Siblings Vaughn and Nicole Alexander, Nickiel's uncle and Shai's aunt, sat courtside observing it all. Their kids who grew up together, who played countless games on the playground, were going back and forth in a crucial clash.

"It feels like you've got to wake up and pinch yourself to make sure the dream's not gonna be over," Vaughn said. "But when you put so much hard work in, you know it's not a dream."

Vaughn, who helped raise Nickeil, was as conflicted as his shimmering chain suggested.

"I'm cheering for both of them; I can't lie," Vaughn said. "I don't care who wins; I just want them both to play well."

They played well, all right. A career playoff high in points for both.

Pushing the Thunder a victory from the NBA Finals, Gilgeous-Alexander was a rebound shy of a triple double: 40 points (13-for-30), 10 assists, nine rebounds.

An exquisite SGA performance, but not as astonishing — given their respective status in the league — as what his cousin accomplished.

Alexander-Walker's 23 points were seven more than Timberwolves star Anthony Edwards had. Alexander-Walker's six assists tied Edwards for the team high.

"Shai was Shai," Vaughn said. "That's who he is. That's a cool, smooth operator. Nothing bothers him. The game's always in slow motion for him. He's always three or four steps ahead. He's just that kid. And when the game's on the line, you want the ball in his hands."

And Nickeil?

Shai Gilgeous-Alexander hunted for way around his cousin, Minnesota guard Nickeil Alexander-Walker, during Game 2 action in OKC. The cousins grew up in Hamilton, Ontario. NATHAN J. FISH/THE OKLAHOMAN

"Same mentality," Vaughn said. "Played like a boss today as well. Tried everything he could do for his team to win and fell a little bit short."

In addition to draining timely 3s, it was Nickeil, not Jaden McDaniels, who got the SGA defensive assignment more times than not down the stretch.

After the game, SAG walked to the baseline seats to embrace his dad and hug his aunt. This matchup between cousins would live on in family lore.

"We'll definitely have plenty of stories about it," SGA said. ■

WESTERN CONFERENCE FINALS

THUNDER 124 | TIMBERWOLVES 94

GAME 5 • MAY 28, 2025 • OKLAHOMA CITY

WOLVES AT THE DOOR

Minnesota Shown the Exit on a Date Now Worth Cherishing

Joel Lorenzi

Take the spotlight, Sam Presti urged, his palm pointing toward the freshly buffed Oscar Robertson Trophy. Shai Gilgeous-Alexander hesitated. No you, Gilgeous-Alexander bashfully beckoned.

Jalen Williams lurked over their shoulders, weary of their modesty, ushering Presti into SGA's embrace like a forced photo op of father and son. Architect and prodigy. Presti undid the top button of his jet black suit jacket so that he could reach to reel in his franchise star.

Presti loosened. He glared up at the videoboard, wide-eyed with a child's closed-mouth smile. Seemingly unsure what to do, he clapped twice, the rush of Oklahoma City's 124-94 Game 5 series-clinching victory over Minnesota coursing through his veins.

For the first time since 2012, the Thunder was bound for the NBA Finals. Among those hovering over the Western Conference champion trophy, only Presti truly knew what it took. He was there on this day nine years earlier — OKC's last chance at a Finals berth in its building.

That fateful night — May 28, 2016, Game 6 of those Western finals — when Klay Thompson's legacy was built on the backs of the Okies of old. His 41-point nuke spurred the Golden State's comeback from a 3-1 deficit, ripping the soul from a city. From a franchise.

Presti's eyes darted around at what emerged from the rubble. His blueprint, years in the making, stared back at him with a baby face. The pain, the sheer difficulty of building a second contender was absent in the gleeful expressions of these CBA babies.

These young Thunder overwrote the memory of a bitter day.

Much of this core's deepest wounds came during 20-something victory seasons and a second-round loss versus a Mavericks team that no longer existed. Perhaps that worked out for them. This squad, the second-youngest NBA Finals team ever, didn't swallow the experience of being turned away and heartbroken year after year. All the history, the accords that were meant to keep such a young team from pushing this far, didn't consider what the Thunder could become during these playoffs.

Presti built a talented and relatively innocent team, though not a naive one.

Game 5 was won with the culmination of this postseason's teachings. As recently as this series, the Thunder was smacked with a reminder of what it's like when your urgency slipped. It faced the "human nature" of a 3-1 lead all the same.

Jalen Williams and OKC polished off Minnesota in easy fashion to punch their ticket to the NBA Finals. Williams contributed 19 points, eight rebounds and five assists. BRYAN TERRY/THE OKLAHOMAN

The Greatest
THUNDER
8
REID
11
Google

The series-clinching victory became a master class in the art of pressing your heel down on the opposing throat. The Thunder, in all the ways its viewers had become accustomed to, seized the day.

It forced 21 Minnesota turnovers, with 17 of them coming before the fourth quarter. Simple passes to the wing for the Timberwolves looked as difficult as an escape room.

This victory looked like so many of the 80 the Thunder had collected this season. A hailstorm of hands, a relentless spin cycle of torturous ball pressure among Alex Caruso (four steals), Lu Dort (three steals), Gilgeous-Alexander (two steals), Williams (one steal) and Cason Wallace (no steals but as blistering a hell exacted as any).

Minnesota's first-quarter shot chart fittingly looked like a pool of blood.

It shot 3-for-20, missing all but one of its nine 3-point attempts. The Timberwolves' nine first-quarter points were the second fewest allowed in the 1Q in the play-by-play era; Denver's eight points in Game 4 of the Western semifinals against OKC were the fewest.

Anthony Edwards, one of the few who presented the tenacity required in an elimination game, scored 19 points on 18 shots, headbutting the Thunder defense to no avail.

"Fifteen puppets on one string," he called them.

Gilgeous-Alexander had been the true puppeteer. The MVP of this season and now of these Western finals looked as comfortable as he had in any series.

He finished with 34 points, eight rebounds and eight assists, on top of making 14 of his 25 shots. He was responsible for 24 of the Thunder's 26 first-quarter points.

The Thunder led by 33 at half. It never lifted the boot, a quality that crystallized something like an Infinity Stone during this postseason. Denver taught it to not loosen its grip. Minnesota showed it how to keep it there.

"We beat the (expletive) out of everybody in the beginning of the year, for the most part, off energy and vibes," Alex Caruso said. "And then through the middle of the season, we started figuring out how we had to execute discipline, details. The last stretch of the season, (we) put it all together."

Jalen Williams completed perhaps his best series yet with 19 points, eight boards and five assists. Chet Holmgren swatted away the Timberwolves' half-hearted comeback efforts, with three blocks to go with his 22 points and seven rebounds.

The ghost of Klay Thompson never thought to howl through the bowels of the Paycom Center. Wallace or Caruso might have somehow managed to pinch him from the air and exorcise him.

Ghostbusters, Jokic-conquerors, record-breakers. This "uncommon" team, as Daigneault loved to call it, had pushed the boundaries. For a rebuild, for a contender. For what could be achieved in a small market.

For what's in reach in little 'ol Oklahoma City. ■

Shai Gilgeous-Alexander helped the Thunder swing into the NBA Finals with 34 points, seven rebounds and eight assists in the Game 5 blowout. BRYAN TERRY/THE OKLAHOMAN

StateFarm
SUNDAES
SUNDAES
NBA
THUNDER
2

NBA FINALS

PACERS 111 | THUNDER 110

GAME 1 • JUNE 5, 2025 • OKLAHOMA CITY

'A 48-MINUTE GAME'

Thunder Falls Victim to Haliburton's Late-Game Sorcery

Joel Lorenzi

Chet Holmgren neared a record for how long humans could clench their jaw. For 8 minutes, 15 seconds, so few words escaped his grinding teeth.

He settled into his postgame seat, flummoxed by a stunning 111-110 Game 1 defeat, with flames in his eyes and the visage of a man who had seen gore. If looks could kill, his would do so serially.

He chewed on the bitter end of the paradox that saw the Indiana Pacers steal Game 1 of the NBA Finals. The Thunder, this millennium's most handsy and incessant defense, was bound to rear its insensitive head. But these Pacers, immune to double-digit deficits — and apparently double-digit turnovers — had often found themselves riding comebacks off into the sunset.

The Thunder controlled every second of Game 1. All but one.

With 2:52 to play, OKC led by nine points. Then came the 12-2 Indiana run to finish. The Thunder shot just 7 of 19 in the fourth, a quarter-long offensive shrug topped off by closing with a small lineup. Then came another signature Tyrese Haliburton moment in a postseason full of them, this time a leaning jumper that gave the Pacers their first lead of the night with 0.3 seconds to play.

And it was that look from Haliburton — tongue poking through his bite, eyes of anticipation, follow-through dangling — that had taken aback the teams forced to bear witness to his late-game prowess.

"It is a 48-minute game," said MVP Shai Gilgeous-Alexander, who finished with 38 points on 30 shots. "(The Pacers) teach you that lesson more than anybody else in the league, the hard way."

At least a handful of Indiana's victories in these playoffs had been out of a bank vault, thrown in duffels like the robberies they were. Game 1 marked the fifth comeback from a 15-point deficit for the Pacers, the most of any team since 1998.

The last team to erase such a deficit in the fourth quarter of a Finals game and win? Rick Carlisle's 2011 Dallas Mavericks.

For a week, the Thunder watched the tendencies. It sought the common thread among all of Indiana's victories of this nature in hopes of avoiding such a fate.

"The common denominator is them," Thunder coach Mark Daigneault said. "That's a really good team. Credit them for not only tonight but their run. They've had so many games like that that have seemed improbable. They just play with a great spirit, they keep coming, they made plays, made shots.

Shai Gilgeous-Alexander was Game 1's leading scorer with 38 points, but the Thunder became the latest team to fall victim to Tyrese Haliburton's late-game heroics. SARAH PHIPPS/THE OKLAHOMAN

Loves
OKLAHOMA
CITY
2

"They deserved to win by a point."

Emphasis on *a point.* Not a full possession. Certainly not double digits. The Thunder led by 12 at halftime, having forced the most turnovers of any team in any Finals half in history. The Pacers had more turnovers (19) than field goals (15).

Entering this series, Indiana was branded by ball control. Entering the second half, the soundtrack to its possessions was Benny Hill's theme, a cycle of offensive dysfunction for a team meant to be immune to it.

The Pacers were ripped on drives. They were crowded all over the floor. Center Myles Turner, with six turnovers, appeared exasperated with the level of contract thrown his way.

But OKC scored just 11 points off a total of 24 turnovers, minced meat for a team that averaged 23.8 points off turnovers entering Game 1. Indiana's final turnover came with 9:45 to play. And while the turnovers slowed (just five in the second half), the Pacers' hope hardly did.

In a duel of firm identities, Indiana stuck around longest. It shot 47.6% from the field and made 46.2% of its 39 3-point attempts.

Aaron Nesmith, a two-way gunner who had helped shape this Pacers run, drilled a heavily contested 3 with just under three minutes left to make the slow burn run truly smoke. Soon after, Andrew Nembhard reached in SGA's bag for a size-up and step-back 3 to further the notion.

The Pacers lived long enough to see their depth swing the game. Turner, at one point nearly ripping his locks out amid the sea of OKC's defenders, finished with 15 points and nine rebounds, a plus-8. Nesmith drilled three 3s. Obi Toppin, a plus-13, knocked down five. Nembhard essentially shut out SGA with the game on the line.

In the final 23 seconds, Gilgeous-Alexander sized up Nembhard, eventually bumping and grinding his way to a midrange jumper. The 15-footer was a fine shot by his standards. With a chance to put the Thunder up three points, he leaned back and misfired.

These Pacers never needed the door opened. Only the window ajar.

"It wasn't like they won the game," center Isaiah Hartenstein said. "It felt like we lost the game."

This feeling boiled in Holmgren at least once these playoffs. After a Game 1 loss to Denver, in which he missed the free throws that allowed Aaron Gordon to steal the show, the big fella's arms reached for his head. There was disbelief in his walk off the floor.

In Game 1, the 7-foot-1 Holmgren shrunk. He and All-Star Jalen Williams, both of whom helped drown Minnesota last round, totaled 23 points on 8-for-28 shooting (Williams scored 17 to Holmgren's six).

In that fateful loss to the Nuggets, this Thunder team saw as an inflection point. Holmgren had walked away in disbelief. This time, his resting expression did the talking. The feeling, familiar as it might be, struck as harsh as the first time.

"It counts the same as when we lost by 40 in Minnesota in the last series," Alex Caruso said. "Counts the same as when we lost by two or three at Denver in Game 3 that series. It's all worth one. It's the silver lining of it.

"But at the same time, it's a loss. If we don't recognize that and feel, if it doesn't hurt right now, you're not frustrated with it, obviously there's something wrong with you." ■

OKC's Carson Wallace couldn't believe that Indiana point guard Tyrese Hamilton nailed a 21-foot shot with 0.3 seconds left in Game 1. Wallace had chased him on the play but could not corral him. BRYAN TERRY/THE OKLAHOMAN

Love's
OKLAHOMA
CITY
22
OKC

NBA FINALS

THUNDER 123 | PACERS 107

GAME 2 • JUNE 8, 2025 • OKLAHOMA CITY

NOT ON OUR WATCH!

Late Haliburton Heater Scares Fans But Does No Harm

Jenni Carlson

Tyrese Haliburton hit a little floater a couple of minutes into the fourth quarter, and a murmur rippled through Paycom Center. There was displeasure, but with the Thunder still up three touchdowns, the faithful found it hard to be too concerned.

But on the next Pacers possession, Haliburton pulled up from the top of the key and ripped the cords.

The murmur this time was louder.

And when the Indiana star drove to the basket unencumbered and threw down a dunk a few moments later, the noise from Thunder fans graduated to a moan laced with anxiety and a sprinkle of panic.

Two nights after Haliburton struck the Thunder with a kill shot, everyone knew what was possible in Game 2. It's like having a cobra in the corner. Even though Haliburton stayed there coiled and quiet for three-plus quarters, he was rising up, threatening to sink deadly fangs into the Thunder.

The only thing that stopped his attack was Rick Carlisle.

With four minutes left in the game, Carlisle pulled his starters even though Haliburton had scored a dozen points in a little over five minutes and sliced the Thunder lead to the point that full-fledged panic was starting to ripple through Paycom Center. And the lead was still 17 points!

As fast as Haliburton fried, the Pacers were just as quickly cooked without him on the floor.

Thunder 123, Pacers 107.

On a night Oklahoma City bounced back from a Game 1 gut punch, it drew even with Indiana in the NBA Finals for several reasons. Better shooting. More scoring from Jalen Williams and Chet Holmgren. Big-time bench production from Aaron Wiggins and Alex Caruso. Keeping both feet on the gas.

But as much as anything, this Thunder bunch won the most crucial game in its existence because of how it handled Haliburton and the rest of the Pacers' offense for three-plus quarters. That fourth-quarter heater was a reminder (as if anyone in Thunder blue needed it) just how combustible he could be.

A reminder, too, of how spectacularly the Thunder held him in check.

"He's a very, very good player," Thunder reserve Kenrich Williams said. "Not sure why people say he was overrated, but he's a very good player, man, and we had a lot of different bodies

Jalen Williams and the Thunder responded to the stunning Game 1 loss by keeping the Pacers at bay late in the 123-107 win. BRYAN TERRY/THE OKLAHOMAN

Health
McCONNELL
9

thrown at him. Just try to slow him down."

Through three quarters, the Thunder did that as well as anyone could expect.

Haliburton went into the fourth quarter with only five points, three rebounds and four assists. He had more turnovers (three) than baskets (two).

"They have a lot of different guys who can guard the ball, fly around," Haliburton said. "They are really physical, force the officials to let us play a little more. ... I think I've had two really poor first halves. I just have to figure out how to be better earlier in games."

Frankly, his end-of-the-third stat line in Game 1 wasn't much different than what it was in Game 2. That night, he had 10 points on 4-for-9 shooting, eight rebounds, five assists and three turnovers.

"Give a lot of credit to Lu," Caruso said of fellow defensive Doberman Lu Dort. "I think he matched up with most of (Haliburton's) minutes. Lu is accepting the challenge. ... He knows the role he needs to play for us to have a chance to win this series and pick up that trophy at the end. He's doing a good job of it."

That point of attack was vital against Haliburton, and the Thunder picked him up early. Whether it was Dort or Caruso or someone else, they were in front of Haliburton as soon as he crossed midcourt, if not sooner.

"They're not the type of style where you're just keying in on one player, just because of the way they play," Thunder coach Mark Daigneault said. "They're more a conceptual team. You have to be kind of a conceptual defense against them. If you do that, I think it has a downstream effect on everybody."

Carlisle described the Indiana offense as an ecosystem.

"We've got to score enough points to win the game," he said, "but who gets them and how they get them? Not important."

That's why playing great defense against Haliburton required playing great defense on the four guys who are on the court with him. Yes, the Pacers had six guys besides Haliburton who scored in double figures, but only two of them did so shooting better than 50% while three had multiple turnovers.

Their efficiency was meh. Credit the Thunder defense.

"We have to play to our principles," Holmgren said. "We've been working on them all year. We can't just forget who we are."

Foundational basics like communication and execution were critical.

"It's really loud in there," Holmgren said of Paycom Center. "We wouldn't want it to be any other way — the fans bring us a lot of energy — but you really have to communicate when it's loud, especially when somebody's up-guarding the ball. They can't see everything behind them. They're trusting you to communicate with them.

"Whoever's guarding the screener kind of, whether they're in coverage or something else, they've got to trust the people behind them to communicate with them what's going on, trust everybody is going to be in the right spots, try to execute over and over again."

That loud Paycom Center crowd got a little restless in the fourth quarter when Haliburton came out of his coil, hissing and spitting and seeking flesh for his fangs. But because the Thunder didn't fall into the Pacers' snake pit, didn't take a hit here and a bite there, there would be no kill shot. ■

Coming off the bench in the NBA Finals, center Isaiah Hartenstein scored only three points in Game 2, but he contributed eight rebounds and four assists. He would start the final four games of the series. NATHAN J. FISH/THE OKLAHOMAN

THUNDER
2
Loves
THUNDER
55
OKC

NBA FINALS

PACERS 116 | THUNDER 107

GAME 3 • JUNE 11, 2025 • INDIANAPOLIS

'STARTS WITH ME'

Indiana Forces Six Turnovers from SGA, Takes the Series Lead

Jenni Carlson

Shai Gilgeous-Alexander caught the ball with Andrew Nembhard charging toward him. A screen freed the Thunder superstar momentarily, and he dribbled toward one of his comfort spots, the free-throw line.

He could stop and pop. He could pull up off the dribble. He could even create his own adventure as he so often did, making highlights almost as frequently as baskets.

Any of those options would have been acceptable with the Thunder trailing midway through the fourth quarter in Game 3 of the NBA Finals.

But instead, as Tyrese Haliburton closed quickly on Gilgeous-Alexander and Nembhard chased him down, SGA opted to pick up his dribble and put himself in a spin cycle, pivoting but taking one too many steps.

Turnover.

A traveling call late in the fourth quarter of an NBA Finals game?

From the MVP?

Really?

If you want to understand why the Thunder lost 116-107 to the Pacers in Game 3 and put itself in an extremely precarious position heading into Game 4, that play explains it.

"They were aggressive," Gilgeous-Alexander said. "They were high in the pick-and-rolls. They were more aggressive, more forceful. ... We've got to apply that pressure back, especially if you want to beat a team like that on the road.

"Starts with me."

The Thunder wasn't the aggressor. Ditto for SGA.

There haven't been many times this season, or for the past few seasons, that you could say that about Gilgeous-Alexander. Even though he plays with an unhurried pace and unflusterable style, make no mistake — he is the aggressor. He decides where he's going on the floor. He chooses how he's going to attack.

But in Game 3, he didn't dictate.

The Pacers did.

The result?

Gilgeous-Alexander scored 24 points but only hit 9 of 20 shots and got to the free-throw line just six times.

Worse, though, he committed six turnovers. That's how many times he turned the ball over in the Thunder's last three games combined, and the last time he committed that many giveaways, most of us still had our holiday decorations up.

Credit the Pacers for the defense they played against Gilgeous-Alexander. Even though every Indiana player had a hand in it, Nembhard

With 2:35 left in Game 3, Indiana's Aaron Nesmith all but tackled Alex Caruso on a breakaway to the basket. OKC wanted a flagrant foul on review but didn't get it. Caruso made two free throws to cut the deficit to six points at 110-104, but the Thunder never could draw closer down the stretch. GRACE SMITH/INDYSTAR

Love's
OKC

and reserve Ben Sheppard had the primary responsibility.

So, what was their secret?

"Well, they are giving it their absolute, full-capacity effort all the time," Pacers coach Rick Carlisle said. "We have to look at the fouls — maybe there's some that are avoidable — but look, with him, he's the MVP.

"You've just got to try to make it difficult."

So, did the Pacers cook up something new defensively against Gilgeous-Alexander? Carlisle is a brilliant coach, so did Indiana find a miracle defense that has eluded every other NBA coach over the past few years?

"I didn't think they really changed their schemes very much," Thunder coach Mark Daigneault said. "I just thought they were sharper with the physicality and the pressure. Their physicality was stronger than our force in a lot of those possessions. Not all of them.

"Obviously, we had really good stretches of the game, but not enough good stretches of the game to stack up to a win on the road."

One adjustment the Pacers did make, though, was on the pick-and-roll. They were picking up Gilgeous-Alexander closer to the midcourt line, something they hadn't done in the first two games of the series, and that meant the defenders were above the screen.

That action caused a reaction.

"When you come off (the screen)," Gilgeous-Alexander said, "you've got to go backwards."

That put him into predicaments near midcourt a few times. And even when there wasn't a double team or a problem dribbling out of trouble, the Pacers were forcing the SGA and the Thunder to change their rhythm. Maybe they had to start their action later in the shot clock. Or change their point of attack.

There's a counter, of course, to that counter.

"If we're more aggressive in the pick-and-roll and setting it up, then we get a better angle," Gilgeous-Alexander said. "Things like that usually come down to who throws the first punch."

The Pacers threw a lot of punches in Game 3, and now, the Thunder finds itself staggered. After losing the opener on a last-second shot, it not only rallied but also showed itself to be the dominant team in Game 2.

Now, however, the Thunder faces a near must-win scenario. Losing Game 4 and going down 3-1 in the series doesn't mean it's over, but winning three in a row, including one of those at Indiana, would be extremely difficult.

Winning Game 4 was crucial.

"You've got to be the more forceful team, for sure," Gilgeous-Alexander said.

And as he indicated, it started with him.

But play again like he did in Game 3, and this series might end with him, too. ■

Shai Gilgeous-Alexander leaped to defend Pacers guard Bennedict Mathurin, who erupted for 27 points on 9-for-12 shooting from the field, 2-for-3 from beyond the arc and 7-for-8 from the line. CHRISTINE TANNOUS/INDYSTAR

INDIANA
00
Loves
THUNDER
2
OKC

NBA FINALS

THUNDER 111 | PACERS 104

GAME 4 • JUNE 13, 2025 • INDIANAPOLIS

FROM CULT HERO TO SUPERHERO

Caruso's 20 Points, Five Steals Lead OKC's Must-Have Comeback

Jenni Carlson

Alex Caruso already has cult-hero status sewed up with the hustle and the headband.

But these NBA Finals should have us thinking bigger. More grandiose. More gravitas. The Thunder veteran has been so important — and never was he more critical than in Game 4, a 111-104 comeback that salvaged the series and the season — that the cult hero is becoming more of a superhero.

So, is there a character he thinks appropriate?

"We'll just do Robin," he said, a twinkle in his eyes, "because that's the only one I can probably make some similarities to and because I got better players around me that are doing more."

Now, that first part is right. Caruso has lots of Robin qualities. The wiry builds. The cerebral approaches.

But players doing more than Caruso?

Difficult to see that.

"If you want to win basketball games," Thunder superstar Shai Gilgeous-Alexander said, "you have a guy like that on your team."

On a night the Thunder rallied from a double-digit deficit in the third quarter and outscored the Pacers by 14 points in the fourth quarter, Oklahoma City not only regained home-court advantage in these Finals but turned this into a best-of-three series with two of those games at Paycom Center.

Securing the biggest victory in franchise history took contributions from lots of players. SGA scoring 15 points in the last five minutes of the game. Lu Dort fighting over screens and setting the tone in the fourth quarter. Chet Holmgren finding himself switched onto guards repeatedly in the final frame and getting misses. Jalen Williams staying aggressive and getting to his spots.

But in a blue-collar, dogfight of a game, no one was any more important than Caruso.

Being blue-collar?

Sticking his neck into the fight?

Caruso has made a career out of those very things.

"He's a competitive monster," coach Mark Daigneault said. "He's proven that time and again over his career, certainly in these playoffs."

He has been so good in the postseason that we've figured time and again that he had reached peak Caruso. A plus-minus of plus-30 without taking a single shot against Memphis? Surely, nothing will top that.

Then came 20 points and five 3-pointers in the opener against Denver.

And the plus-40 performance when he guarded Nikola Jokic in Game 7.

And the kibosh he helped put on Julius Randle in the Western Conference finals.

And another 20 points in that massive Game 2

Alex Caruso's 20 points shifted the balance of Game 4 as the Thunder mounted a second-half comeback. KYLE TERADA/IMAGN IMAGES

SIAKAM

victory against the Pacers in the NBA Finals.

"What makes Alex very good is that he's able to figure out what we need and be that," Williams said. "Makes big shots. Obviously, defense speaks for itself. He's just really smart. He's kind of like our fill-in.

"He does a really good job of seeing what the game needs and then doing it at 100%, which is hard to do since he's like 100."

Williams snickered. Caruso might be the old guy in the Thunder locker room, but no one was more respected than the 31-year-old.

"He's just our glue on that end of the floor," Williams said.

Everyone knew about Caruso's defense, but in Game 4, the Thunder wouldn't have won without his offense.

With the Thunder offense struggling to find its footing in the first half, Caruso helped stabilize. A drive that netted a floating bank shot and free throw. Another drive and floating bank. A steal that created an easy transition basket.

Caruso had seven points in the first quarter, behind only Williams' 12.

"The way that Indiana is playing, it's leaving opportunities for supplemental offense for other guys," Caruso said. "Game 3, I don't think I was aggressive enough. I think I made a couple bad reads on the perimeter. I don't think I tested the paint enough. I just didn't feel like I was doing the same amount of work that I did in Game 1 and 2, where I found success and we found success as a team."

In the third quarter, Caruso had another huge stretch offensively.

After the Thunder cut the Pacers' lead to two with just under five minutes left in the quarter, Obi Toppin hit back-to-back 3s. The Gainbridge Fieldhouse crowd roared. The game felt like it was teetering on the edge.

Caruso pulled the Thunder back from the brink, getting to the free-throw line, then hitting a 3.

"He does whatever it takes on any given night," Gilgeous-Alexander said. "Whether it's making shots, whether it's deflections, a steal, a block, whether it's a rebound, he does whatever it takes every night.

"I've said this before, but he has a championship ring for a reason. It's no coincidence. He knows what it takes. He put the work in. He's proving it every night. But he's a big-time performer. Big-time teammate. Big-time winner."

Caruso, who earned his ring with the 2020 Lakers, finished with 20 points on 7-for-9 shooting, five steals and a plus-14.

Competing is like breathing for Caruso.

"I want to win," he said. "I don't care if it's pickup in September before training camp. I don't care if it's Game 45, 50, before All-Star break, if it's the Finals and you're down 2-1, I want to win. That's what I'm focused on."

He admits that early in his career, his ability to have an impact on winning games in the NBA was limited. He relied largely on his defense, his tenacity, his determination.

But the past few years, he has spent his offseasons working to expand what he can do.

Everyone in the Thunder locker room recognizes what he has contributed. As he lingered outside the celebration swirling on the Indiana hardwood after the final buzzer, his teammates found him.

One after another, they came for high-fives and hugs.

Still, Caruso talks like he's the fortunate one.

"These guys, to be able to do it without a lot of experience and without being in that moment before," he said, "this is their first NBA Finals, down 2-1 on the road, down 10 at one point in the game, just answering, throwing punches, throwing punches. That can't get overlooked. That's an impressive feat."

Sorta like a cult hero morphing into something more — something super. ■

Chet Holmgren's decision to attack the basket drew the attention of Indiana's Tyrese Haliburton, Pascal Siakam and Myles Turner. Holmgren finished 14 points and 15 rebounds. GRACE HOLLARS/INDYSTAR

SIAKAM
43

NBA FINALS

THUNDER 120 | PACERS 109

GAME 5 • JUNE 16, 2025 • OKLAHOMA CITY

'THE COURT IS SHAKING'

OKC Fans Raise the Decibels as Thunder Closes in on Title

Joe Mussatto

Jalen Williams yelled a defensive coverage to Lu Dort, but Dort couldn't hear his teammate. And it's not like they were trying to communicate from across the court.

"He was two feet away," Williams said, "and we can't hear each other."

Anyone in Paycom Center could relate. For three hours, it was the loudest place on planet Earth. A concrete kettle that whistled louder than ever as the Thunder topped the Pacers 120-109 in Game 5 of the NBA Finals to draw one victory from the franchise's first world championship.

"It feels like the court is shaking when we're here," Williams said. "They give us that boost we need."

All the cliche home-court advantages applied in Game 5:

- Role players rose to the occasion. Aaron Wiggins and Cason Wallace combined to shoot 7-for-11 from 3-point range. Neither made a 3-pointer in Games 3 and 4 at Indianapolis. The Thunder shot 44% from beyond the arc as a team. Oklahoma City shot better from behind the arc than it did inside of it.
- The Thunder got out and ran, outscoring the Pacers 17-13 in fast-break points.
- OKC forced 22 turnovers, outscoring Indiana 32-9 in points off miscues.

Paycom Center, as it did in Game 5, brings out the best in the Thunder.

"Unreal," coach Mark Daigneault said. "I mean, they've been unreal forever. They just put the wind at our back.

"We have to give them a reason to. We have to play with the type of togetherness and competitiveness and spirit that they can relate to, which I thought we did tonight."

The Thunder was 10-2 at home in the playoffs, outscoring opponents by 20.7 points per 100 possessions. Its two losses were on shots at the buzzer. On the road, the Thunder was 5-4 in the playoffs, getting outscored by 5.0 points per 100 possessions.

That's a 25-point swing in the Thunder's home/road splits. Even if OKC lost Game 6 at Indianapolis, it would have the ultimate advantage coming home for a Game 7.

Thunder fans were loud — not exactly breaking news, I know — but they cranked things to another level for Game 5. Some stood for the entire game. Armed with their fan banners, they made Paycom Center feel like it had a pulse.

Jalen Williams celebrated a 3-pointer during the fourth quarter of Game 5 in Oklahoma City. NATHAN J. FISH/THE OKLAHOMAN

Love's
OKLAHOMA
CITY
8
OKC

After a Jalen Williams dunk. *Roars.*

After a Wallace 3-pointer. *Roars.*

After an SGA and-1. *Roars.*

After another Dort defensive stop. *Roars.* (Dort, by the way, hounded Pacers star Tyrese Haliburton into an 0-of-6 shooting night. Haliburton had the same number of baskets as superfans Thundor and Brick Man.)

"When we're not playing well, they help us," Shai Gilgeous-Alexander said. "When we're playing well, they keep us going. They've been great all year. Tonight was no different. We expect that from them."

The noise was unrelenting even when the game got nervy. Like when Pacers forward Pascal Siakam drilled a 3-pointer to cut the Thunder's lead to two points with 8:30 to play. OKC had led by as many as 18.

But after Williams responded with a massive 3-pointer and Wallace followed with a pick-six slam, the party was back on. Pacers coach Rick Carlisle had no choice but to call a time-out.

Of course it was Williams, always the match to the crowd's kerosene, who starred in Game 5. Williams, already an All-Star and All-NBA player, made his full-on arrival on the national stage. Williams dropped 40 points, six rebounds and four assists. He was more than just a sidekick to Gilgeous-Alexander, who had a not-so-shabby 31 points and 10 assists.

"Definitely a special thing to be part of Oklahoma, the team, how well the fans embrace us," Williams said. "For them to be outside the (airport) gate at 2, 3 a.m. and greet us, be excited, it's super dope.

"That's special. That's something we're definitely playing for. We always have in the back of our mind how lucky we are and I am to be here."

Fueled by those fans, a Thunder championship was finally within reach.

"One more win, one more win, one more win," Thunder fans chanted as they spilled out of Paycom Center, which, on this night, was the loudest place on Earth. ■

Fans at Paycom Center went wild after Cason Wallace swiped a pass, raced down the court ahead of Tyrese Haliburton and threw down a dunk for a 100-93 lead. In only 17:28, Wallace managed 11 points and four steals. SARAH PHIPPS/THE OKLAHOMAN

Loves
OKLAHOMA
CITY
22

NBA FINALS

PACERS 108 | THUNDER 91

GAME 6 • JUNE 19, 2025 • INDIANAPOLIS

'WE SUCKED TONIGHT'

On the Brink of a Title, Thunder Gets Run of the Building

Joe Mussatto

Mark Daigneault waited as long as he reasonably could have before calling his first time-out. It was as if he didn't want to intervene in the action, instead waiting for his team to show some spunk. To hush the Indiana crowd and halt the Pacers' run on its own.

That wait would be an indefinite one.

Game 6 was all Indiana: 108-91 Pacers.

"The way I see it is, we sucked tonight," said Shai Gilgeous-Alexander, his analysis unimpeachable.

The Pacers played with desperation. The Thunder played as if it had a fallback option — a Game 7 wild card tucked away in the recesses of the visitor's locker room. Which was true of course, but boy oh boy, that's a dangerous game to play. Anything and everything was on the table in a Game 7. Not closing things out in Game 6 left the Thunder susceptible to the whims of the ball bouncing a certain way. Of Obi Toppin or Aaron Nesmith or Ben Sheppard catching fire from deep. Of the Thunder going cold. Of a missed call.

"We have one game for everything, for everything we've worked for, and so do they," SGA said. "The better team Sunday will win."

The Thunder was the better team, OKC had been the NBA's best team all season, but Game 7s weren't much for past sample size. We've reached the single-elimination portion of the season.

You couldn't help but wonder how much the safety net of a Game 7 resulted in the Thunder's Game 6 no-show.

"The human element didn't creep in for me until we got blown out," Jalen Williams said. "I didn't start thinking about Game 7 until we walked off the floor."

Gilgeous-Alexander, who had eight turnovers, turned the page before then.

"One game for all the marbles," SGA told his teammates, in audio captured on ABC's broadcast, in the fourth quarter when Game 6 had long been put to bed.

Game 7 *was for all the marbles.* But for the Thunder, *so was Game 6.* The Thunder could have taken the title then and there in Indianapolis, but the champagne bottles stayed corked. Maybe now OKC might win the title in front of its home crowd, which might be the best of both worlds, but there was also the possibility of, well, you know.

"Obviously that's frustrating," Chet Holmgren said. "It's not fun. Nobody is happy right now. But you can't let the emotions kind of sidetrack you from what we need to do leading up to and during the game coming up.

"We've had wins and losses throughout the playoffs, so it's kind of a similar mentality: Turn the page, don't forget just what happened, but see where you can be better and try to apply it going forward."

One of the lessons of this series: Count out the Pacers at your peril.

Pacers defenders swarm Shai Gilgeous-Alexander, who had eight turnovers in the Thunder's Game 6 loss.
CHRISTINE TANNOUS/INDYSTAR

Tyrese Haliburton looked awfully spry for a guy hobbled by a calf injury. How about that sequence just before halftime? Haliburton stole a Williams pass (one of the Thunder's 21 turnovers) and tight-roped the sideline before whipping a no-look, spinning dime to Pascal Siakam for a slam.

It was a highlight that capped a horrific second quarter for the Thunder, one in which OKC was outscored 36-17. The Pacers led by 22 at halftime and that was that. The 10-2 lead the Thunder sprinted out to was but a distant memory.

OKC had no answers to Indiana's runs. No antidotes for the affliction that had been T.J. McConnell. All McConnell did was tally 12 points, nine rebounds, six assists and four steals. Toppin, another Indiana reserve, had a team-high 20 points.

No amount of time-outs was changing the tenor of Game 6.

"You don't get an unlimited number," Daigneault said. "We have to have the ability to play through some things. I tried to stop the play when I could.

"But all the way around, we just weren't where we needed to be tonight. Our ability to course correct in games is important. We've done that well. We have to do that in these games. It's a 48-minute game."

There's only one 48-minute game left to play. And this one, as SGA said, was for all the marbles. ■

NBA FINALS

THUNDER 103 | PACERS 91

GAME 7 • JUNE 22, 2025 • OKLAHOMA CITY

THUNDEROUS!

In Year 17, OKC Finally Reigns Supreme

USA TODAY Network

After 17 seasons of Thunder basketball, it finally rained in Paycom Center.

Blue-and-orange confetti fell from the rafters as the final buzzer sounded. That solidified the OKC Thunder's 103-91 victory over the Indiana Pacers in Game 7 of the NBA Finals.

Indiana fans took shelter by heading toward the exits, leaving nothing but a sea of blue in the stands. OKC's players shielded themselves by throwing on T-shirts with large text across the front: NBA CHAMPIONS.

The Thunder capped a dominant season — 68 victories, No. 1 on defense, No. 3 on offense — with the franchise's first championship since relocating from Seattle in 2008. OKC became the second-youngest team to win a championship. It also was the sixth different champion in the past six seasons.

Point guard Shai Gilgeous-Alexander, the MVP of the regular season, scored 29 points, dished out 12 assists, grabbed five rebounds and was selected the MVP of the Finals. He became the 11th player to be a double MVP. The last player to win those awards in the same season was LeBron James with the Miami Heat in 2013. Among the others were some of the biggest names in the league's history: Michael Jordan (four times), Larry Bird (twice), Magic Johnson, Shaquille O'Neal and Kareem Abdul-Jabbar.

For the Finals, SGA averaged 30.3 points, 5.6 assists, 4.6 rebounds and 1.9 steals, plus he shot 91.4% from the free-throw line.

"The most impressive part is the group that did it," Gilgeous-Alexander said. "Our togetherness on and off the court (and) how much fun we have, it made it so much easier. It made it feel like we were just kids playing basketball. It was so fun."

Game 7, though, wasn't easy. Even with the Pacers losing their superstar, Tyrese Haliburton, with 4:55 left in the first quarter. The game was tied at 16, and Haliburton, nursing a strained calf for several games, had buried three 3-pointers.

Haliburton's right leg gave out when he attempted to drive, near the same spot on the court where he stumbled in Game 5. But the result was far worse this time. He was flat on his stomach, pounding the hardwood court with his right fist. Instant replay showed a pop near his calf.

Jalen Williams helped the Thunder put an exclamation point on its championship run with 20 points, four rebounds and four assists in the Game 7 win over the Pacers. BRYAN TERRY/THE OKLAHOMAN

Loves
THUNDER
8

THUNDER
2
Loves
INDIANA
9

Later, John Haliburton, Tyrese's father, told ESPN sideline reporter Lisa Salters that his son suffered an Achilles tendon injury.

"All of our hearts dropped," Pacers coach Rick Carlisle said.

Gilgeous-Alexander, the closest player to Haliburton, tried to comfort him.

"My heart dropped for him," SGA said. "I couldn't imagine playing the biggest game of my life and something like that happening. It's not fair. But competition isn't fair sometimes."

Despite losing Haliburton, the Pacers never truly went away and even led 48-47 at the half. The score was 56-all with 8:32 left in the third quarter.

But Haliburton's absence was too much to overcome. Carried by its stars and depth, OKC outscored Indiana 25-12 for an 81-68 lead heading into the final quarter and pushed its advantage to 90-68 with 7:41 left in the game.

Still, the Pacers trimmed the deficit with 10 points in the final three minutes before the Thunder could close it out.

"There was no surrender," Carlisle said. "It was all defiant fight to the end."

Jalen Williams scored 20 points and Chet Holmgren 18 for the Thunder. Also in double figures were Alex Caruso and Cason Wallace with 10 points apiece. Bennedict Mathurin led the Pacers with 24 points and 13 rebounds, and T.J. McConnell and Pascal Siakam each scored 16 points.

The Thunder won the turnover battle 23-8 and converted Indiana's mistakes into 32 points.

"It comes down to the moments and who is willing to make winning plays on both ends of the floor," Gilgeous-Alexander said. "I relish those moments, love the moments, good or bad. When I was a kid shooting at my driveway, I'd count down the clock for those

Pesky T.J. McConnell and the equally pesky Pacers could slow Shai Gilgeous-Alexander at times but could never stop him. He capped his season as the MVP of the Finals, powering Oklahoma City to its first NBA championship. BRYAN TERRY/THE OKLAHOMAN

NBA
THUNDER
7
Loves
OKC
NEMBHARD
2

moments. Now I get to live it. It's a blessing, it's fun, and I relish it."

OKC began this season as the youngest team in the NBA. It ended with a championship, an MVP winner in Gilgeous-Alexander, two All-Stars, two All-NBA players, two All-Defensive players, the league's best record and the league's top-rated defense.

OKC also will enter the offseason with all of its rotational players under contract, and it had two picks (No. 15 and No. 24) in the draft. Then there was the boatload of future picks that general manager Sam Presti had saved for a rainy day.

Now, the rest of the league could be in for some rainy days. The perfect storm appeared to be brewing in Oklahoma City.

Yes, it's difficult to build a dynasty in today's NBA. The roster restrictions and financial penalties limited what teams could do. Surveying the NBA landscape, though, the Thunder appeared positioned to make it happen.

"I haven't even thought that far ahead," Gilgeous-Alexander said. "But, yeah, we definitely still have room to grow. That's the fun part of this. So many of us can still get better. There's not very many of us on the team that are in our prime or even close to it.

"We have a lot to grow, individually and as a group. I'm excited for the future of this team. This is a great start, for sure. ... Couldn't have imagined it any other way." ■

— Justin Martinez, Jacob Unruh, Jeff Zillgitt, Gregg Doyel, Josh Peter and Jeff Patterson contributed.

Chet Holmgren was the backbone of a suffocating Thunder defense that forced 23 turnovers and held the Pacers to a paltry 91 points. Holmgren stuffed the stat sheet with 18 points, eight rebounds and five blocks. BRYAN TERRY/THE OKLAHOMAN

A TITLE OF HIS OWN

Presti Relishes the Process, Keeps Memento from the Results

June 22, 2025 | Joe Mussatto

Sam Presti rolled a champagne cork between his fingers long after the bottles had been popped. It was a modest token compared to the shiny Larry O'Brien Trophy, to the championship ring he soon will be fitted for, but a meaningful one just the same. And Presti had exactly the place to put it.

A small glass case in Presti's closet contains three other corks, one for each of the three Spurs championships he was a part of in 2003, 2005 and 2007. Titles that helped Presti, at age 29, land a job as general manager of the Seattle SuperSonics. Eighteen years later, Year 17 in Oklahoma City, Presti had another cork to add to his collection.

A title of his own. The first Thunder championship in team history.

Two hours after the Thunder's 103-91 Game 7 victory against the Indiana Pacers, Presti, soaked in champagne and sweat, finally had time to exhale.

"Still sinking in a little bit," Presti said a few steps from the confetti-littered court. "Just very, very happy for our players. They have prioritized all the right things and have come together as a group of men in a way that has allowed us to achieve something that's really unique for the city and community.

"That's the thing I thought about the most, is how happy I am for them."

If you couldn't tell, the last thing Presti wanted to talk about was himself. It made him squirm.

Presti obsessively preached process-over-results, but this result — an NBA title — was the only thing the basketball boy genius had yet to conquer. With it, he had proved *something,* hadn't he?

Presti kept his pivot foot, dishing the credit back to his team.

"I'm extremely happy that we have achieved this because I think it's a great testament to a lot of people and their hard work," he said. "I'm much more focused and much more drawn to *how* it took place than actually *what* took place.

"I look back and I think about the fact that Chet (Holmgren) missed a large part of the season. We were playing without a center up until December. We've had a lot of different experiences within the year, some challenges throughout the year that ultimately made us better. I'm thrilled with the outcome, but I'm savoring the process that led to that."

The process, the rebuild, started six years ago, in the summer of 2019, when the Thunder traded Paul George for Shai Gilgeous-Alexander and a

Thunder general manager Sam Presti was part of the front office for three championships with the San Antonio Spurs but saved his biggest achievement for his 17th year in Oklahoma City, where he helped bring the city its first NBA title. BRYAN TERRY/THE OKLAHOMAN

Champions
25
OKC
CITY

future pick that became Jalen Williams. The depths of the Thunder's rebuild lasted just two seasons — one of which netted the Thunder the No. 2 pick in the draft. The pick that became Holmgren.

It was around that Big Three — SGA, J-Dub and Chet — that the Thunder was built. With a coach in Mark Daigneault now recognized as one of the best in the business. After a second-round exit a season ago, Presti bolstered the roster by acquiring Alex Caruso via trade and Isaiah Hartenstein in free agency.

Presti, the architect, had designed an all-time squad. A championship team. The second-youngest in NBA history.

"Yeah, Presti!!! Yeah, Sam!!!" Holmgren shouted at his general manager during one of Presti's postgame TV hits.

The speed in which this all happened was unintentional. The steps in which the Thunder got here? Each was precisely planned by Presti. Implemented on the court by Daigneault. Executed by Gilgeous-Alexander, the MVP.

"Things take longer than you think they should, and then when they happen, sometimes they happen faster than you think they could have," Presti said. "And we never really looked at time or specific periods or benchmarks. Really just tried to focus on building a team that could be sustainable and not take shortcuts.

"It unfolded this way because of the players and their professionalism, their rate of learning. Their rate of learning has outpaced their experience. I thought the team got better throughout the postseason from game to game — even in the losses. I think the team improved from Game 6 to Game 7. They've demonstrated the ability to learn and apply those things quickly. That's a credit to them and the coaches."

And it's a credit to Presti for bringing them all together. For hiring the right coach. For assembling not just a deep and talented roster, but one in which the individual parts and personalities meshed.

"Just seeing their relationships and how much those relationships have grown over the last two, three years, that brings me a lot of joy," Presti said.

A joy that could be seen as he hugged his players. As he laughed with Daigneault and wrapped his arms around Clay Bennett, the man who hired him.

In the locker room after the game, Presti used his free hand to dap up dozens of staffers. In his other hand was a Miller Lite.

And somewhere along the way, someone — Presti couldn't remember who — handed him a champagne cork.

A cork Presti clung to for what it represented. ■

While Sam Presti was selective in detailing his franchise building plans for the Thunder over the years, he was thoughtful and reflective when describing the championship journey after Oklahoma City won Game 7 to secure the trophy. NATHAN J. FISH/THE OKLAHOMAN

NBA
NBA
OKC

BRYAN TERRY/THE OKLAHOMA